A

Reformed Baptist

Manifesto:

The New Covenant

Constitution of the

Church

Samuel E. Waldron

with Richard C. Barcellos

Reformed Baptist Academic Press
Palmdale, CA

Requests for information should be sent to:
Reformed Baptist Academic Press
37104 Bridgeport Ct.
Palmdale, CA 93550
rbap@sbcglobal.net
www.rbap.net

Printed in the United States of America.

ISBN 0-9760039-0-2

The will of our Lord Jesus Christ is that His people would be one (John 17). That is part of the "not yet" that we anticipate so eagerly. Yet, it must also be a distinct element of our striving "now". The divisions within the Evangelical community cannot be simply accepted by us without a humble attempt to pursue unity in meaningful ways. This book may sound unhelpful in this endeavor by its title. In actuality, however, it is a serious contribution to the oneness of Christ's people in our generation! Mr. Waldron addresses perhaps the most serious divisions of biblical interpretation among Evangelicals today. The purpose is not to win one for Reformed Baptists, but to promote our (Reformed Baptist) understanding of Scripture in the vital area of covenant theology. As a Reformed Baptist pastor, I am happy to commend this for the Church universal to read and study.

Gary W. Hendrix
A pastor of Grace Reformed Baptist Church
Mebane, NC

****

It is with great pleasure that I recommend this work to be read by all students of theology. The New Covenant as prophesied in the Old Testament is often dealt with lightly in terms of its fulfillment in the New Testament. Sam Waldron has done us a favor by clearly explaining the meaning of the original prophecy in context and establishing its fulfillment according to New Testament statement. His gracious exposure of others' errors reveals that they basically misinterpret the meaning of the New Covenant and its present fulfillment in the Church of Jesus Christ. His explanation of the implications of the New Covenant, rightly understood, provide a guide and blueprint for establishing biblical churches today. It provides a *Manifesto*, rooted in the very meaning of the New Covenant.

Fred A. Malone, Ph.D.
Pastor, First Baptist Church, Clinton, LA
Author of *The Baptism of Disciples Alone: A Covenantal Argument for Credobaptism Versus Paedobaptism*

****

Of the many interfaces of theology, one fascinating area is the relationship of the New Covenant to the Old. What aspects of the Old Covenant were strictly dispensational, that is, applying to the Jews of Israel during the time they as a nation were living in that land and had a unique covenant relationship with God? What truths of the Old Testament have a permanent binding authority on the New Testament people of God? These studies are a modest step towards clearer thinking about revealed truth. May it be the first of many. We all need such light and direction as are to be found in these pages.

Geoffrey Thomas
Pastor, Alfred Place Baptist Church, Aberystwyth, Wales
Associate Editor of the Banner of Truth magazine
Author of *Ernest C. Reisinger: A Biography*

****

The centuries old dispute concerning the nature of the church and all the important related issues may seem so complex as to defy clarification. Waldron's insightful discussion cuts through so much of the confusing rhetoric and allows the reader to see clearly the key elements of the differing positions in light of the teaching of God's Word regarding the New Covenant. Many will be blessed by this fresh approach.

James R. White, Th.D.
Phoenix Reformed Baptist Church, Phoenix, AZ
Alpha and Omega Ministries

****

Table of Contents

Preface

This book's title may at first glance seem to promise more than it delivers. It is not intended as a manifesto of all the distinctives of confessional Reformed Baptists. That is contained, substantially, in our confession of faith, the Second London Confession of Faith 1677/1689. This book, however, presents a very focused manifesto concentrating on one element (a major one) of Reformed Baptist theology as it relates to and, in some instances, is in opposition to the views of others. Our focus will be, as intimated by the subtitle, *The New Covenant Constitution of the Church*.

This book finds its origin in a series of sermons preached many years ago. Much has transpired on theological fronts since the delivery of those sermons. An attempt has been made, therefore, to update the arguments where needed and add contemporary comment on various theological movements within American Evangelical Christianity.

It is hoped that this humble effort will assist confessional Reformed Baptists in articulating their distinctives and help others understand why we believe what we do concerning the New Covenant.

A word is in order about the authorship of this

little book. The author line reads Samuel E. Waldron
with Richard C. Barcellos. I preached the original
four messages upon which this book is based. The
editorial help given by Richard was so extensive that
I felt it completely proper to include his name in the
author line. I am grateful for the wonderful kindness
and amazing appreciation that he has shown for those
sermons by both the original request to publish them
and the extensive labors he has expended upon them
in order to make them fit for publication.

Samuel E. Waldron
July 2004

Introduction

It is the conviction of this author that confessional Reformed Baptist churches[1] reflect the major distinctives of the New Covenant. In other words, what confessional Reformed Baptists endeavor to be is stated clearly in the terms of the New Covenant. The purpose of this study, therefore, is to set before you a Reformed Baptist Manifesto by means of an examination of the New Covenant as the Constitution of the Church. This assertion may seem arrogant. It is hoped, however, that the reader will simply permit the New Covenant to speak for itself and see the relevance and appropriateness of such a claim.

Though differences with other Christians will be discussed, let it be clearly and emphatically stated at the outset that confessional Reformed Baptists stand with many Reformed and Dispensational brothers on the essential issues of the Christian faith. We gladly stand shoulder to shoulder with all those who hold to the plenary inspiration, inerrancy, authority, and sufficiency of Scripture. We are very glad that many of our Reformed and Dispensational brothers are standing firm on justification by faith alone in Christ alone. We

---

[1] For our purposes, a confessional Reformed Baptist church refers to any local church subscribing to the Second London Confession of Faith of 1677/1689 (2nd LCF).

are glad to affirm our unity with all who are standing firm against the onslaughts of Open Theism. Though we differ on the details of the New Covenant, we are one on these issues and many others essential to the Christian faith.

The phrase "New Covenant" is used explicitly five times in the New Testament. There are at least five more times in which clear allusions to it occur. This, however, does not adequately reveal the all-importance of the New Covenant in the Bible. The last 27 books of our Bibles are called the New Testament. This phrase is an alternate translation of the New Covenant. In one sense, the New Testament is the New Covenant. That is to say, the Scriptures of the New Testament are the Scriptures of the New Covenant, just as the Scriptures of the Old Testament are the Scriptures of the Old Covenant. This in no way takes the Old Testament out of the hands of Christians. Just as the Old Testament has to do with the establishment and implications of the Old Covenant, so the New Testament has to do with the establishment and implications of the New Covenant.

This way of speaking about the two parts of our Bibles is not merely traditional. In 2 Corinthians 3:14, the Apostle Paul, having spoken in this very context of the New Covenant (2 Cor. 3:6), speaks of "the reading of the old covenant." By this phrase he intends the consecutive, public reading of the Old Testament Scriptures in the Jewish synagogues. Not only does the New Testament frequently and explicitly refer to the New Covenant, the Scriptures of the New Testament in a sense are the New Covenant. The subject of the New Covenant is, obviously, of vital importance for all Christians.

It is amazing to realize that despite all of the attention to the New Covenant in our New Testaments, there is only one passage in the entire Old Testament where this phrase occurs. That pivotal passage will be the focal point of this study. That passage is Jeremiah 31:31-34.

The premise of this study is intimated in its subtitle: *the New Covenant Constitution of the Church.* To state that premise plainly, the New Covenant is the Constitution of the Church of Christ. In other words, what the Constitution of the United States of America is to our country, what the *Magna Carta* is to the British Commonwealth, that the New Covenant is to the Church of Christ.

The term covenant is undoubtedly one of the most important words in the Bible, used over 280 times in the Old Testament and over 30 times in the New Testament. It has been deservedly the focus of much learned discussion. One issue important for this study that this discussion has established is this: A covenant in the Bible, among other things, is the formal or legal basis of some relationship. For instance, Malachi 2:14 ("she is your companion and your wife by covenant") speaks of the marriage covenant as the formal, binding, legal basis of marriage. Similarly, the Old or Mosaic Covenant was the formal, legal, basis for the national existence of Israel. It stated the terms on which Jehovah had formally taken the nation of Israel for His bride. For instance, Ezekiel 16:8 says, ""Then I passed by you and saw you, and behold, you were at the time for love; so I spread My skirt over you and covered your nakedness. I also swore to you and entered into a covenant with you so that you became Mine," declares the Lord GOD." This Old Covenant is explicitly compared to and contrasted with the New Covenant in Jeremiah 31.

This is why the New Covenant is the Constitution of the Church. Though written church constitutions are permissible for the sake of administration, the premise for this study is that the New Covenant is itself the ultimate, formal basis and legal rule of the Church. This study, therefore, will be spent in establishing and opening up this premise from Jeremiah 31.

Due to the issues at stake and the attempt to present a Reformed Baptist Manifesto this study will be somewhat polemic. As the study progresses, we will be discussing the views of others with which we differ. As we unearth confessional Reformed Baptist distinctives grounded in the New Covenant, some differences with other Evangelical Christians will be exposed. We will conduct ourselves in the interest of truth, intending no malice.

Here is the outline that will be followed:

- *The New Covenant Constitution of the Church and Dispensationalism*
- *The New Covenant Constitution of the Church and Antinomianism*
- *The New Covenant Constitution of the Church and Arminianism*
- *The New Covenant Constitution of the Church and Paedobaptism*

The approach to these issues will be as follows. During the course of our examination of the New Covenant, confessional Reformed Baptist doctrine will be established and then compared and contrasted with Dispensationalism, Antinomianism, Arminianism, and

Paedobaptism. The result will be a Reformed Baptist Manifesto based on the New Covenant as the Constitution of the Church.

CHAPTER ONE:
The New Covenant Constitution of the Church and Dispensationalism

It first must be established that the New Covenant is, indeed, the Constitution of the Church, especially since some have denied it such relevance. In this chapter, we will be laying much of the foundation upon which is built the rest of this study.

In Jeremiah 31:31-34, we read:

"Behold, days are coming," declares the LORD, "when I will make a new covenant with the house of Israel and with the house of Judah, not like the covenant which I made with their fathers in the day I took them by the hand to bring them out of the land of Egypt, My covenant which they broke, although I was a husband to them," declares the LORD. "But this is the covenant which I will make with the house of Israel after those days," declares the LORD, "I will put My law within them, and on their hearts I will write it; and I will be their God, and they shall be My people. And they shall not teach again, each man his neighbor and each man his brother, saying, 'Know the LORD,' for they shall all know Me, from the least of them to the greatest of them," declares the LORD, "for I will forgive their iniquity, and their sin I will remember no more."

The question we must answer at this point is: Does, in fact, this passage have anything to do with the Church? Is the New Covenant really the Constitution of the Church? This question is particularly crucial because, as hinted above, it is denied by an important segment of Evangelical Christianity. The approach at this point will be to open up the validity of the premise (i.e., the New Covenant is the Constitution of the Church) under three headings: Its Denial; Its Defense; and Its Difficulty.

Its Denial: The promise of the New Covenant does not apply to the Church

The denial that the New Covenant is strictly relevant to the Church comes from a movement that dominates much of American Christianity. That movement or system of interpretation is commonly known as Dispensationalism. It is, perhaps, most well known as that system of interpretation popularized by *The Scofield Reference Bible.*

This system, in its classic statement, denies that the New Covenant is fulfilled in (or is the Constitution of) the Church. Before this assertion is proven, it needs to be briefly clarified. This must be done because there may be a few who complain that, by claiming Dispensationalism denies the New Covenant is fulfilled in the Church, it is being misrepresented.

In recent years, different versions of what is called Progressive Dispensationalism have been put forth. Not a few Evangelical scholars are keenly aware of the biblical inadequacies of Classic Dispensationalism. These scholars, rather than admit the inadequacy of Dispensationalism per se, have attempted to re-define it. Having re-defined it, they can continue to claim allegiance to their revered system.

There is, however, a problem with those who object that Dispensationalism is being misrepresented. If scholars are allowed to define Dispensationalism any way they please, then it can become anything they want it to be. Some modern dispensationalists re-define their system so that those who are not dispensational may be categorized as dispensational. There is something wrong with your definition when it can turn anti-Dispensationalism into Dispensationalism. When one's definition of an apple is so broad that by that definition tomatoes are apples, there is something inadequate about that definition. One wonders if what constitutes Dispensationalism today will be what constitutes Dispensationalism tomorrow.

These scholars may be compared to an antique car buff that has the rusty old frame and body of a Model T sitting in his back lot. He drops a Mitsubishi four cylinder engine into it, a Mercedes transmission, Porsche wheels, and Michelin tires. In general, he so overhauls the thing that, when he is finished, the only item made before 1990 in that automobile is the frame and part of the body. Then he comes to you and claims to own a Model T Ford. What's the problem? He owns a Model T Ford only in a highly qualified sense of the word. Much of contemporary Dispensationalism is so but only in a highly qualified sense of the word.

A second response to those worried that Dispensationalism is being misrepresented is that, however they may define it in the atmosphere of academia, it is not the kind of Dispensationalism believed in the pews of churches across America and the world. What is being spoken of primarily is the

Classic Dispensationalism commonly believed in America.[1]

It can be proven that Classic Dispensationalism denies the New Covenant is fulfilled in the Church by quoting some of the most well known teachers of this system of thought. J. Dwight Pentecost, in his classic treatise on dispensational eschatology entitled *Things to Come*, says the following, "...the new covenant of Jeremiah 31:31-34 must and can be fulfilled only by the nation Israel and not by the Church ....the covenant stands as yet unfulfilled and awaits a future, literal fulfillment."[2] Another former professor of Dallas Theological Seminary, Charles C. Ryrie, succinctly states his view this way: "The New Covenant is not only future, but millennial."[3] A third major exponent and well-known teacher of Classic Dispensationalism reiterates this point. John Walvoord asserts, "...the premillennial position is that the new covenant is with Israel and the fulfillment in the millennial kingdom after the second coming of Christ."[4]

This denial is neither incidental, nor unimportant for Classic Dispensational Premillennialism. Ryrie asserts that Dispensationalism has three essentials. According to Ryrie, one of those essentials is, "A dispensationalist keeps Israel and the Church distinct ...

---

[1] It will be pointed-out below that even Progressive Dispensationalism fails to adequately deal with the promise of the New Covenant and its fulfillment in and application to the Church.

[2] J. Dwight Pentecost, *Things To Come* (Grand Rapids: Zondervan Publishing House, 1964, 1979), 124, 125.

[3] Charles Caldwell Ryrie, *The Basis of the Premillennial Faith* (Neptune, NJ: Loizeaux Brothers, 1975), 112.

[4] John Walvoord, *The Millennial Kingdom* (Findlay, OH:Dunham, 1958), 209.

a man who fails to distinguish Israel and the Church will inevitably not hold to dispensational distinctions."[5] Elsewhere he says, "If the Church is fulfilling Israel's promises as contained in the new covenant or anywhere in the Scriptures, then premillennialism is condemned."[6] In a context assuming the Church fulfills the New Covenant, Pentecost acknowledges, "If the Church fulfills this covenant, she may also fulfill the other covenants made with Israel and there is no need for an earthly millennium."[7]

Not only does Classic Dispensational Premillennialism deny that the Church fulfills the New Covenant, it must deny this or utterly collapse. This conclusion is obvious, even to adherents of that system. Classic Dispensationalism cannot admit that the church fulfills the New Covenant made with Israel. This would constitute a failure to keep Israel and the Church distinct and separate. It would be to admit that Israel and the Church are in some sense one and the same. According to Ryrie and Pentecost, this would destroy Premillennialism (and all forms of Dispensationalism). They are, of course, absolutely correct.

Its Defense: The promise of the New Covenant does apply to the Church

The defense of our premise that the New Covenant

---

[5] Charles Caldwell Ryrie, *Dispensationalism Today* (Chicago: Moody Press, 1965), 44-48.

[6] Ryrie, *Premillennial Faith*, 105, 106, 111. There are other reasons for the "condemnation" of Premillennialism. See the author's *The End Times Made Simple* (Amityville, NY: Calvary Press, 2003).

[7] Pentecost, *Things to Come*, 116.

is fulfilled in and by the Church is neither hard nor complicated. We will simply look at the use that the New Testament makes of Jeremiah 31:31-34 and seek to answer this question: What does the New Testament teach about the fulfillment of the New Covenant? We will examine seven passages to obtain the answer.

Luke 22:20

In Luke 22:20, Jesus said, "This cup which is poured out for you is the new covenant in My blood." This is the last supper eaten by Jesus and the Apostles in which the Lord's Supper was instituted. The Apostles were, according to Ephesians 2:20, the foundation of the Church. Jesus speaks of the cup He shares with His Apostles as "the new covenant in My blood." That is to say, the cup was the outward symbol of the New Covenant. Their drinking of the cup clearly symbolizes their having a part in Christ's blood and the blessings it procures.

1 Corinthians 11:25

In 1 Corinthians 11:25, Paul says to the Corinthian church, "In the same way He took the cup also, after supper, saying, "This cup is the new covenant in My blood; do this, as often as you drink it, in remembrance of Me."" This is the definitive passage on the subject of the Lord's Supper in the New Testament. It demonstrates that the events of Luke 22:20 were intended to institute a continuing ordinance for the Church (cf. 1 Cor. 11:17-22 and 1:1, 2). That being the case, every time a Christian takes the cup which Christ Himself identified as "the new covenant in My blood," he is saying, "I have a part in the New Covenant, in its blessings, in its rules, in it as the Constitution of

Christ's Church."

2 Corinthians 3:6
Paul says:

> Not that we are adequate in ourselves to consider
> anything as coming from ourselves, but our
> adequacy is from God, who also made us adequate
> as servants of a new covenant, not of the letter, but
> of the Spirit; for the letter kills, but the Spirit gives
> life. (2 Cor. 3:6)

The reference of this passage to Jeremiah 31:31-34
cannot be evaded. In Jeremiah 31:33 we read of God
writing His law on the hearts of His people, just as we
do in this context. In 2 Corinthians 3:3, we read, "being
manifested that you are a letter of Christ, cared for by
us, written not with ink, but with the Spirit of the living
God, not on tablets of stone, but on tablets of human
hearts." Gentile Corinthians, believers and church-
members, had, therefore, the blessings promised in the
New Covenant found in Jeremiah 31.

But verse 6 is even more significant. Paul identifies
himself, the Apostle to the Gentiles, the Apostle of the
Church, as a servant of "a new covenant." Now the
question must be pressed: How could the Apostle to
the Gentiles be a servant or minister of the New
Covenant if that covenant is not fulfilled in the Church,
but is "future and millennial"?

Hebrews
The New Covenant and Jeremiah 31 have their
most concentrated New Testament exposition in the
Epistle to the Hebrews. It has been argued that this
letter and its references to the New Covenant are

irrelevant for the Church of the Gentiles. Wasn't Hebrews written, it is asked, to Jews?

It may be that most of those to whom Hebrews was originally addressed were, as to their national origin, Jews. That does not, however, subtract from the significance of this letter for the Christian Church and the issues before us. This is true for at least three reasons. *First*, since Hebrews is part of the New Testament and was written after the close of the Old Testament dispensation, the privileges it bestows and the duties it lays upon Christian Jews cannot be limited to Jews. This would be to re-erect the dividing wall between Jew and Gentile that, by His cross, Christ has torn down. This point will become even more evident as we begin to look at the actual passages in Hebrews. *Second*, this is underscored by the fact that Hebrews was written mainly to Christian Jews. These Christian Jews were being exhorted not to apostatize back into Judaism. *Third*, those being addressed were members of Christian Churches. They are, for instance, warned not to forsake their assembling together (Heb. 10:25) and exhorted to "Obey your leaders, and submit to them; for they keep watch over your souls" (Heb. 13:17). This is plainly a reference to the elders of those Christian Churches of which, it is assumed, they are members.

Hebrews 8:1, 6-13

> Now the main point in what has been said is this: we have such a high priest, who has taken His seat at the right hand of the throne of the Majesty in the heavens (Heb. 8:1)

But now He has obtained a more excellent ministry, by as much as He is also the mediator of a better covenant, which has been enacted on better promises. For if that first *covenant* had been faultless, there would have been no occasion sought for a second. For finding fault with them, He says,

"BEHOLD, DAYS ARE COMING, SAYS THE LORD,
WHEN I WILL EFFECT A NEW COVENANT
WITH THE HOUSE OF ISRAEL AND WITH THE HOUSE OF
    JUDAH;
NOT LIKE THE COVENANT WHICH I MADE WITH THEIR
    FATHERS
ON THE DAY WHEN I TOOK THEM BY THE HAND
TO LEAD THEM OUT OF THE LAND OF EGYPT;
FOR THEY DID NOT CONTINUE IN MY COVENANT,
AND I DID NOT CARE FOR THEM, SAYS THE LORD.
"FOR THIS IS THE COVENANT THAT I WILL MAKE WITH
    THE HOUSE OF ISRAEL
AFTER THOSE DAYS, SAYS THE LORD:
I WILL PUT MY LAWS INTO THEIR MINDS,
AND I WILL WRITE THEM UPON THEIR HEARTS.
AND I WILL BE THEIR GOD,
AND THEY SHALL BE MY PEOPLE.
"AND THEY SHALL NOT TEACH EVERYONE HIS FELLOW
    CITIZEN,
AND EVERYONE HIS BROTHER, SAYING, 'KNOW THE
    LORD,'
FOR ALL SHALL KNOW ME,
FROM THE LEAST TO THE GREATEST OF THEM.
"FOR I WILL BE MERCIFUL TO THEIR INIQUITIES,
AND I WILL REMEMBER THEIR SINS NO MORE."

When He said, "A new *covenant*," He has made the first obsolete. But whatever is becoming obsolete and growing old is ready to disappear. (Heb. 8:6-13)

The writer here quotes Jeremiah 31:31-34 as

speaking of that better covenant of which our high priest is the minister and mediator. This certainly implies that the New Covenant promised in Jeremiah was inaugurated by Christ and is currently being fulfilled.[8]

Hebrews 9:14, 15

...how much more will the blood of Christ, who through the eternal Spirit offered Himself without blemish to God, cleanse your conscience from dead works to serve the living God? And for this reason He is the mediator of a new covenant, in order that since a death has taken place for the redemption of the transgressions that were *committed* under the first covenant, those who

---

[8] Classic Dispensationalism argued that the writer of Hebrews never intended to teach that Israel's New Covenant was now operative. Pentecost says, "Thus, in Hebrews 8 the promise of Jeremiah is quoted only to prove that the old covenant, that is the Mosaic, was temporary from its inception, and Israel never could trust in that which was temporary, but had to look forward to that which was eternal. Here, as in Hebrews 10:16, the passage from Jeremiah is quoted, not to state that what is promised there is now operative or effectual, but rather that the old covenant was temporary and ineffectual and anticipatory of a new covenant that would be permanent and effectual in its working. It is a misrepresentation of the thinking of the writer to the Hebrews to affirm that he teaches that Israel's new covenant is now operative with the Church" (Pentecost, *Things to Come*, 125, 126). Pentecost does say that the New Covenant was instituted by Christ's blood, but that "these [ethnic Israelites] to whom it was primarily and originally made will not receive its fulfillment nor its blessings until it is confirmed and made actual to them at the second advent of Christ ...There certainly is a difference between the institution of the covenant and the realization of the benefits of it" (Pentecost, *Things to Come*, 126, 127).

have been called may receive the promise of the eternal inheritance. (Heb. 9:14, 15)

Here Jesus is presented as the mediator of the New Covenant that conveys to its recipients cleansing and redemption from sin. These recipients are described as "those who have been called" (v. 15). The New Testament teaches that God is calling both Jews and Gentiles to the promise of the eternal inheritance (Rom. 9:24). If you have been called, then Jesus is the mediator of the New Covenant for you, and you partake in the New Covenant and its blessings.

Hebrews 10:10-19

By this will we have been sanctified through the offering of the body of Jesus Christ once for all. And every priest stands daily ministering and offering time after time the same sacrifices, which can never take away sins; but He, having offered one sacrifice for sins for all time, SAT DOWN AT THE RIGHT HAND OF GOD, waiting from that time onward UNTIL HIS ENEMIES BE MADE A FOOTSTOOL FOR HIS FEET. For by one offering He has perfected for all time those who are sanctified. And the Holy Spirit also bears witness to us; for after saying,
"THIS IS THE COVENANT THAT I WILL MAKE WITH THEM
AFTER THOSE DAYS, SAYS THE LORD:
I WILL PUT MY LAWS UPON THEIR HEART,
AND UPON THEIR MIND I WILL WRITE THEM," *He then says,*
"AND THEIR SINS AND THEIR LAWLESS DEEDS
I WILL REMEMBER NO MORE."
Now where there is forgiveness of these things, there is no longer *any* offering for sin.
Since therefore, brethren, we have confidence to enter the holy place by the blood of Jesus, (Heb. 10:10-19)

The promise of the New Covenant that God will remember our sins and iniquities no more (Jer. 31:34) is here seen as fulfilled through the sacrifice of Christ. Because of that promise, we as Christians "have confidence to enter the holy place" (v. 19). Thus, every Christian, Jew or Gentile, who enters the holy place in private prayer or in public worship by the blood of Christ, does so because he has been made a partaker of the New Covenant and its blessings.

Hebrews 12:22-24

> But you have come to Mount Zion and to the city of the living God, the heavenly Jerusalem, and to myriads of angels, to the general assembly and Church of the first-born who are enrolled in heaven, and to God, the Judge of all, and to the spirits of righteous men made perfect, and to Jesus, the mediator of a new covenant, and to the sprinkled blood, which speaks better than *the blood* of Abel. (Heb. 12:22-24)

In coming to Mount Zion, we have also come to the "Church of the first-born" (v. 23). These blessings are, however, conveyed to us in and through the things to which we have come named in verse 24. The things mentioned in verse 24 occupy a climactic place in the passage because it is by means of them that all the other blessings are conveyed. In other words, it is through Jesus, the mediator of the New Covenant and the sprinkled blood, that such as we are may come to Mount Zion and the Church of the firstborn. Thus, a place in the Church is possessed in virtue of a relationship with the mediator of the New Covenant.

Conclusion

Every New Testament use of Jeremiah 31:31-34 relates it to a present fulfillment in the Church. Conversely, there is no justification anywhere in the New Testament for seeing its fulfillment as future and millennial (either in whole or in part). There is, on the other hand, every reason to see it as the Constitution of the Church in the present age. Just remind yourself of what we have seen. The Savior of the Church is the mediator of the New Covenant. The Apostle of the Church is a servant of the New Covenant. The origin of the Church is owed to the blessings of the New Covenant. The very ordinances of the Church are signs of the New Covenant. Thus, we must conclude, the New Covenant is the Constitution of the Church.

Its Difficulty: The difficulty of applying the New Covenant to the Church

Despite the clarity of the witness of the New Testament on this subject, a problem may remain in the mind of the reader. Despite all this evidence, there may be for some a nagging doubt. You may be asking: Does not Jeremiah 31 say that the New Covenant was to be made with the house of Israel and the house of Judah? How can it be, then, that the New Covenant is fulfilled in the mainly Gentile Church?

The simple answer to that question is that the Church is Israel. Or, to state it more precisely, if the New Covenant is currently being fulfilled, it must be made with and constitute a New Israel. Far from Classic Dispensationalism's severing of the Church and Israel, the Bible teaches that the Church is the continuation of Israel in a new form in the new age. There is much evidence for this assertion, but we will examine only the three most important passages in the New Testament which prove that the Church is the New Israel. This is contrary to all forms of Dispensationalism, as we shall see.[9]

Galatians 3:29

Paul says, "And if you belong to Christ, then you are Abraham's offspring, heirs according to promise." Paul climaxes his argument in chapter three of Galatians with the assertion that the true seed of Abraham, the true Son of God, was Jesus the Christ (Gal. 3:16). But that is not all he says. Those who are in Christ, united to Him by faith, are also Abraham's seed and, thus, spiritual Jews and true Israelites.

All of this may seem like spiritualizing to some. It must be pointed out, therefore, that the Church is the seed of Abraham and the Israel of God only because it is, as Galatians 3:29 plainly says, in union with One who was truly the physical seed of Abraham.

---

[9] Though Progressive Dispensationalism sees the New Covenant fulfilled in the Church, it still demands a future millennium for many prophesies of the Old Testament to find their fulfillment. This does not deal adequately with the fact that the Israel of Old Testament prophecy is the Church of the Lord Jesus Christ. Since the promise of the New Covenant in Jeremiah applies to the Church, then all other Old Testament prophecies apply to the Church (cf. 2 Cor. 6:16-7:1 where Old Testament promises of the New and Davidic Covenants [see also Lk. 1:69; Acts 2:22-36 and 15:12-18] and Gal. 3 [see also Lk. 1:54, 55 and 72, 73] where promises relating to the Abrahamic Covenant are applied to the Church). No future millennium is needed. All Old Testament prophecies concerning the future of Israel on this earth are being and will be fulfilled by the Church, whether in this age or in the age to come.

Romans 11:16-24

> And if the first piece *of dough* be holy, the lump is
> also; and if the root be holy, the branches are too.
> But if some of the branches were broken off, and
> you, being a wild olive, were grafted in among
> them and became partaker with them of the rich
> root of the olive tree, do not be arrogant toward
> the branches; but if you are arrogant, *remember
> that* it is not you who supports the root, but the
> root *supports* you. You will say then, "Branches
> were broken off so that I might be grafted in."
> Quite right, they were broken off for their
> unbelief, but you stand by your faith. Do not be
> conceited, but fear; for if God did not spare the
> natural branches, neither will He spare you.
> Behold then the kindness and severity of God; to
> those who fell, severity, but to you, God's
> kindness, if you continue in His kindness;
> otherwise you also will be cut off. And they also,
> if they do not continue in their unbelief, will be
> grafted in; for God is able to graft them in again.
> For if you were cut off from what is by nature a
> wild olive tree, and were grafted contrary to
> nature into a cultivated olive tree, how much more
> shall these who are the natural *branches* be
> grafted into their own olive tree? (Rom. 11:16-24)

Here Paul likens the people of God to an olive tree.
The root of the olive tree is the covenant promise made
to the Jewish patriarchs. The natural branches are the
Jews. Now what happens when Christ comes? Does
God uproot the old olive tree? Does He plant a new fig
tree beside the old olive tree? Does He perhaps plant a
second olive tree? The answer to all these questions is
a resounding no. This passage plainly teaches that the

same old olive tree continued, but its unbelieving Jewish branches were broken off and new branches, believing Gentiles, were grafted in. What's the point? Classic Dispensationalism teaches that the Church and Israel are distinct, separate, two different peoples of God. The Bible's viewpoint is in stark contrast. It teaches that the Church is not a new olive tree. It is the old olive tree, but with new, believing branches. It is Israel, New Israel. Paul appears completely insensitive to "dispensational distinctions" in this passage.

Ephesians 2:11-13

> Therefore remember, that formerly you, the Gentiles in the flesh, who are called "Uncircumcision" by the so-called "Circumcision," *which is* performed in the flesh by human hands—*remember* that you were at that time separate from Christ, excluded from the commonwealth of Israel, and strangers to the covenants of promise, having no hope and without God in the world. But now in Christ Jesus you who formerly were far off have been brought near by the blood of Christ. (Eph. 2:11-13)

There is a crucial question raised by verse 13. Unto what have the Gentiles been brought near? The answer to this obvious question is also equally obvious. Two considerations put the answer beyond all doubt.

First, they are clearly brought near to those things from which verse 12 says they were previously excluded. What are those things? Among other things, it is, "the commonwealth of Israel."

Second, the transition from being excluded to being included is repeated in Paul's conclusion to this passage in verse 19. Note the "so then" with which verse 19 begins. "So then you are no longer strangers and aliens" (Eph. 2:19). The Gentile fellow-believers are now said to be "fellow-citizens with the saints" (Eph. 2:19). Clearly, the "saints" here mentioned are the Jewish saints. Even more significant is the fact that the word translated "fellow-citizens" is derived from the same root translated "commonwealth" in verse 12. Paul's point is abundantly clear. Believing Gentiles are now, by the work of Christ, full citizens of the nation of Israel.

Conclusion

The New Covenant can be fulfilled in the Church because it is the New Israel of God. And, it must be emphasized, this is not spiritualizing. The head of the Church, the root of the Church, the apostolic foundation of the Church, even all the original members of the Church were Jews.

A radio preacher once asserted that a certain chapter of Acts was "Jewish" ground. There is, however, much more "Jewish" ground in the book of Acts than one chapter. Indeed, the whole New Testament is "Jewish" ground, because the Church itself is in its whole origin "Jewish."

Practical Implications

We have established the validity of our premise that the New Covenant is fulfilled in the Church and is its Constitution. In the process, the Classic Dispensational system of Bible interpretation has been weighed in the balance of Scripture and found wanting. We quoted, you remember, a representative spokesman of this system who said, "He who does not keep the Church and Israel distinct will inevitably not hold to dispensational distinctions. ...If the Church is fulfilling Israel's promises as contained in the new covenant or anywhere in the Scriptures, then premillennialism is condemned."

But the Bible itself refuses to keep Israel and the Church distinct as all forms of Dispensationalism do. We have already seen the position of Classic Dispensationalism on this issue. Now listen to what Robert L. Saucy presents as the view of Progressive Dispensationalism.

> The biblical teaching about the roles of Israel and the Church in history reveals that although they have much in common, they remain distinctively different. Believing Israel and the members of the Church are one in their participation in the eschatological salvation of the new covenant. Because of the relationship to God that this entails, they are equally and together "the people of God." ...In both Testaments, the identity of "Israel" is always the historical people descended from Abraham through Jacob that became a nation. Israel was called to witness God's salvation to the other nations as a nation among nations. The Church, by contrast, is identified in the New Testament as a people called out of *all* nations. In distinction to Israel in her being and witness as a "nation," the Church is called to proclaim the kingdom salvation as individuals and as a community living in the midst of the nations, but not yet in the totality of a "nation." [10]

---

[10]   Robert   L.   Saucy,   *The   Case   for   Progressive*

Jesus, however, said to the Pharisees, "Therefore I say to you, the kingdom of God will be taken away from you, and be given to a nation producing the fruit of it" (Matt. 21:43). Peter calls the Christians he addressed in 1 Peter "A HOLY NATION" (1 Pet. 2:9). From the Bible's perspective, therefore, the Church is the eschatological nation of Israel, reconstituted according to the terms of the New Covenant. Thus, the Bible itself demands that we reject all forms of Dispensationalism at this point. This is, we realize, a blunt assertion. No offense is intended. We are not denying that many sincere and godly Christians have held and still hold to this system. We are not saying that such Christians have not taught many important biblical truths. We are simply asserting that the dispensational system with its peculiar views about the Church and Israel and prophecy is wrong.

There may be some who have never even heard of Dispensationalism, or for whom it is not an issue. What has all of this to say to you? You may be deeply influenced by an error without realizing it or even knowing its name. A warning against an error that our discussion has exposed and one not by any means restricted to dispensationalists is appropriate at this time. *Beware of minimizing the importance of the Church of Jesus Christ.*

Many things in Dispensationalism conspire to minimize or depreciate the importance of the Church in the plan of God. The simple fact that the Church becomes, in older Dispensationalism, one of two distinct peoples of God depreciates its importance. The fact that the really exciting prophetic events have to do

---

Dispensationalism (Grand Rapids: Zondervan Publishing House, 1993), 218.

with Israel deepens the problem. The great prophecies of the Old Testament are not for the Church, but for Israel, according to Dispensationalism.[11] We in the Church age live in a great parenthesis in history when the prophetic clock has stopped ticking. The dispensation of the Church is doomed like all the others to end in abject failure. The visible Church is corrupt, apostate, bound to get worse, and sure to fail. The conclusion of one Classic Dispensational teacher is surely correct if such teaching is true. He said, "Don't polish the brass on a sinking ship!" No wonder many professing Christians regard the Church and local Church membership as an optional or secondary part of their Christian lives. After all, isn't membership in the spiritual, invisible Church sufficient?

We must set over against all such attitudes the teaching of the Bible. The Church is the New Israel. She is the fulfillment of Old Testament prophecy. God has no other age, no other plan, and no other organization through which His kingdom is to be peopled with the nations of the earth. The Church, says Paul, is that people "upon whom the ends of the ages has come" (1 Cor. 10:11). The Church is the fruition of

---

[11] Both Classic and Progressive Dispensationalism teach that the great prophecies of the Old Testament are for Israel in a future millennium (cf. Saucy, *Progressive Dispensationalism*, 221ff.). Once it is acknowledged that the Church is the Israel of Old Testament prophecy, however, there becomes no need for a future millennium for the fulfillment of these prophecies. This is further strengthened by the fact that the New Testament constantly focuses upon the second coming of Christ, the general resurrection, the final judgment, and the New Heavens and the New Earth as the next great prophetic and eschatological events, not the millennium. See the author's *The End Times Made Simple*.

God's "eternal purpose which He carried out in Jesus Christ our Lord" (Eph. 3:11). Thus, Paul cries out, "to Him be glory in the Church and in Christ Jesus to all generations forever and ever. Amen" (Eph. 3:21).

Be solemnly admonished, therefore, not to minimize the importance of the Church. Here are some ways the Church is minimized:

(1) By thinking of it as a mere human institution. The Church is both Divinely originated and Divinely regulated by the New Covenant. Christ established no other institution to carry on His work in the world. There are no other biblically warranted visible manifestations of that institution in the world than local churches.

(2) By sinfully neglecting membership in it. Jesus founded the Church as His New Israel. He expects His people to seek formal citizenship in it. Could it be that the casual attitude of some about Church membership is rooted in a minimizing of the Church of Christ?

(3) By resentment of its authority. Such resentment of biblical accountability to a local Church and its appointed representatives is a form of lawlessness, if the Church is, indeed, at the heart of God's plan for the ages.

(4) By vision-less stagnation in our hopes for it. It is the Church that must evangelize the lost. It is the Church that must plant other churches. It is the Church that must engage in foreign missions. It is the Church that ought to spread the Word through literature, publishing, and bookstores. It is the Church that must prepare men for the Gospel ministry. There are great things to be done, and it is the Church that must

do them.

(5) By pessimistic prayerlessness for its prosperity.
The Church is the appointed manifestation of
the people of God, the inheritance of God, the
Israel of God. It is the apple of God's eye. It is
the focus of the labors of our ascended Lord.
Remember Christ's words, "...I will build My
Church ..." (Matt. 16:18). Churches ought to
pray, labor, and hope as the triumphant Israel
of God.

CHAPTER TWO:
The New Covenant Constitution of the Church and Antinomianism

In this chapter, we will be looking at the New Covenant Constitution of the Church and Antinomianism. The word antinomian simply means against law. There are various types of Antinomians, but in some way or another, all Antinomians deny that the Ten Commandments as a unit are a rule of life for the Christian. Historically, Antinomians have been labeled differently, depending on the type of Antinomianism to which they adhere. Practical Antinomians not only teach against law in the Christian life, they often advocate lawless living. Doctrinal or Moderate Antinomians, however, do not advocate lawless living, but they deny the third use of the law (i.e., the Ten Commandments as a rule for Christian living) or, at best, advocate it but redefine what law means.[1] The movement within Calvinistic Baptist

---

[1] See Francis Turretin, *Institutes of Elenctic Theology* (Phillipsburg, PA: P&R Publishing, 1994), II:141ff., where he discusses the fact that Antinomians deny the third use of the law. See Ernest F. Kevan, *The Grace of Law* (Grand Rapids: Baker Book House, 1976, second printing, February 1983), 22 (n.32), 24, 25, for evidence that those who denied the perpetuity of the Decalogue and hence, the third use of the law, were

circles called New Covenant Theology (NCT), for instance, fits within Doctrinal or Moderate Antinomianism.[2] NCT denies the perpetuity of the Decalogue as a unit under the New Covenant and its function as the epitome of the Moral Law throughout redemptive history. NCT as a movement, however, does abominate Practical Antinomianism, and rightly so. The Ten Commandments function as the epitome of the Moral Law in the Bible, as we will see. Many in our day deny this crucial fact. Many Christians in our day are, therefore, Antinomian in some sense.

This chapter will concentrate on an exposition and application of Jeremiah 31:33. The words, "I will put My law within them, and on their heart I will write it," will be the focus of our attention. We will learn of the place of the Ten Commandments and, thus, the Moral Law under the New Covenant. We will also expose the error of Antinomianism in its various forms. Once again, the terms of the Constitution of the Church, the New Covenant, are sufficient to both confirm us in the truth and expose error. We will ask and answer three questions: About what law is verse 33 speaking?; What

---

labeled as moderately antinomian or doctrinally antinomian, even though considered otherwise virtuous.

[2] See Jonathan F. Bayes, *The Weakness of the Law* (Carlisle, Cumbria, UK: Paternoster Press, 2000), 44-46, where he discusses John G. Reisinger (NCT advocate) in the context of doctrinal antinomianism; Richard C. Barcellos, "The Death of the Decalogue," *Tabletalk*, September 2002, which is a brief discussion of the doctrinal antinomianism of NCT; Richard C. Barcellos, "John Owen and New Covenant Theology," *Reformed Baptist Theological Review*, I:2 (July 2004), 43, 44; and Ian McNaughton, "Antinomianism in Historical Perspective" and James M. Renihan, "Caterpillars and Butterflies," *Reformation Today*, September-October 2003, No. 195, 9-16 and 23-26.

is meant by the writing of that law on the heart?; What is the reason that the law is written on the heart?

About what law is verse 33 speaking?[3]

The clue for resolving this question is found in the contrast and parallel between the Old and New Covenants stated in these verses (cf. vv. 32, 33a, "not like the covenant which I made with their fathers …But this is the covenant which I will make …"). Clearly, there is a contrast in these verses between the Old and New Covenants. But that very contrast assumes and implies a parallel. Let me state the contrast clearly. The Old Covenant was broken because God wrote His law on stone and not on all the hearts of His people. The New Covenant will not be broken, because God will write His law on the hearts of all His covenant people.

The clear contrast here is the place *where* the law is written. In the Old Covenant, the place is on the stone tablets. In the New, it is the fleshy heart. But in this contrast there is also clearly a parallel. In both covenants, God writes His law. The contrast clearly assumes and implies the parallel. The contrast in where the law is written, however, assumes that the law under discussion still has a vital place to play in God's New Covenant.

In light of this clear parallel, we may return to our

---

[3] See Richard C. Barcellos, *In Defense of the Decalogue: A Critique of New Covenant Theology* (Enumclaw, WA: WinePress Publishing), 16-22 and Fred A. Malone, *The Baptism of Disciples Alone: A Covenantal Argument for Credobaptism Versus Paedobaptism* (Cape Coral, FL: Founders Press, 2003), 92, 93 for similar treatments of this crucial verse.

question with a better understanding of its answer. About what law is verse 33 speaking? Two things clearly identify this law.

First, it is the law written by God Himself and by His own finger. This is clear from verse 33, "I will put My law within them, and on their heart I will write it..." But the only law so written was the Moral Law of God as summarized in the Ten Commandments. It is the Ten Commandments, and those Ten Commandments alone, which were written by God Himself and with His own finger.

> Now the LORD said to Moses, "Come up to Me on the mountain and remain there, and I will give you the stone tablets with the law and the commandment which I have written for their instruction." (Exo. 24:12)

> And when He had finished speaking with him upon Mount Sinai, He gave Moses the two tablets of the testimony, tablets of stone, written by the finger of God. (Exo. 31:18)

> And the tablets were God's work, and the writing was God's writing engraved on the tablets. (Exo. 32:16)

> Now the LORD said to Moses, "Cut out for yourself two stone tablets like the former ones, and I will write on the tablets the words that were on the former tablets which you shattered." (Exo. 34:1)

> At that time the LORD said to me, "Cut out for yourself two tablets of stone like the former ones, and come up to Me on the mountain, and make an ark of wood for yourself.

> And I will write on the tablets the words that were on the former tablets which you shattered, and you shall put them in the ark." (Deut. 10:1, 2)

> And He wrote on the tablets, like the former writing, the Ten Commandments which the LORD had spoken to you on the mountain from the midst of the fire on the day of the assembly; and the LORD gave them to me. (Duet. 10:4)

Other aspects of the Old Covenant law, the Judicial and Ceremonial, were written, not by God Himself, but by Moses. "And Moses wrote down all the words of the LORD" (Exo. 24:4; cf. 34:10-27).

Second, it is the law written on stone that is re-written in the New Covenant on the heart of all covenant participants.[4] The emphasis on the place where God's law is written in Jeremiah 31:33 plainly suggests this thought. This is confirmed by the references of the Apostle Paul to this verse in 2 Corinthians 3:1-8. Here Paul uses the very words to speak of the stone tablets in the Septuagint (the Greek translation of the Hebrew Scriptures [LXX]) of Exodus 31:18 and 34:4. The Judicial Law of Israel was not written on stone, but in a book (Exo. 24:3, 4, 7; contrast these verses with v. 12). The Ceremonial Law of Israel was not written on the heart. Only the Moral Law, as epitomized and summarily contained in the Ten Commandments, was written on stone.

---

[4] See Psa. 37:31 and Is. 51:7 for evidence that the law was on the heart of at least *some* Old Covenant citizens. What the New Covenant promises is the law written on the hearts of *all* its citizens.

Conclusion

The law being spoken of in Jeremiah 31:33 is obviously and clearly the Moral Law as summarized in the Ten Commandments, and not the Judicial, nor the Ceremonial Law. It is this law that was written on stone. It is the same law, therefore, that is written on the hearts of all New Covenant believers. It is this law alone that was written by God's own finger on the tablets of stone. Thus, it must be this law alone that is written on the hearts of believers under the New Covenant. Another thought which further confirms the identity of this law is found in Romans 2:14, 15. There is an allusion to Exodus 20 and Jeremiah 31 in the phrase, "the work of the Law written in the hearts" (v. 15). According to this passage, it is in substance the law written on stone in the Old Covenant and re-written on the heart in the New Covenant which at the beginning by creation was written on the heart and conscience of Adam.[5] Where it is not perverted and suppressed, it still expresses itself in the conscience of every child of Adam.

Before we move on, there is one issue that we cannot pass by without addressing. The key to understanding the assertion of Jeremiah 31:33 and, indeed, one of the keys to understanding the whole biblical doctrine of God's law is the distinction

---

[5] NCT denies these crucial points. See the appendix by Richard C. Barcellos, a review of the book *New Covenant Theology,* for further discussion and Richard C. Barcellos, "John Owen and New Covenant Theology," *RBTR*, I:2 (July 2004), 24-30 for evidence that Witsius, Owen, Turretin, and Boston reference Jer. 31:33 in contexts arguing for the perpetuity of the entire Decalogue under the New Covenant. This proves that our exegesis of this text is not novel in the history of Reformed interpretation.

asserted in the 2nd LCF. This distinction is found in almost identical language in both the Presbyterian (Westminster Confession of Faith) and Baptist versions of that Confession. Chapter 19 paragraphs 2-5 state this important distinction this way:

> 2 The same law that was first written in the heart of man continued to be a perfect rule of righteousness after the fall, and was delivered by God upon Mount Sinai, in ten commandments, and written in two tables, the four first containing our duty towards God, and the other six, our duty to man.
> 3 Besides this law, commonly called moral, God was pleased to give to the people of Israel ceremonial laws, containing several typical ordinances, partly of worship, prefiguring Christ, his graces, actions, sufferings, and benefits; and partly holding forth divers instructions of moral duties, all which ceremonial laws being appointed only to the time of reformation, are, by Jesus Christ the true Messiah and only law-giver, who was furnished with power from the Father for that end abrogated and taken away.
> 4 To them also he gave sundry judicial laws, which expired together with the state of that people, not obliging any now by virtue of that institution; their general equity only being of moral use.
> 5 The moral law doth for ever bind all, as well justified persons as others, to the obedience thereof, and that not only in regard of the matter contained in it, but also in respect of the authority of God the Creator, who gave it; neither doth Christ in the Gospel any way dissolve, but much strengthen this obligation.

Many in our day deny this distinction. Both

Dispensationalism and some professedly Reformed theologians want us to think that no Israelite could have seen the difference between moral laws on the one hand, and ceremonial-judicial laws on the other. Now, of course, it is true that the Law of Moses was not color-coded in its original edition with blue for moral laws, yellow for ceremonial laws, and green for judicial laws. Yet, as we have seen, God in other ways made clear that there was a big difference between the Moral Law, as summarized in the Ten Commandments, and the rest of the law of Israel. Passages like the ones quoted above, and many others, make clear that godly Israelites were able to distinguish the Moral from the Ceremonial in Israel's law. One great safeguard against the extremist and imbalanced views of God's law, which abound on every side in our day, is a solid grasp on the biblical and confessional distinction between moral, judicial, and ceremonial laws. It is only when we, understanding the Constitution of Christ's Church, realize that we are also to be guided by what was Moral in the law of Moses, especially the Ten Commandments, that we will have a complete and un-mutilated guide for the Christian life and the Christian Church.

What is meant by the writing of that law on the heart?

The key to understanding this concept is the biblical meaning of the heart. This is an important and broad subject. Two important points about the heart will serve our purposes at this point.

The heart is, *first* of all, the seat and center of our convictions and affections. Proverbs 4:23 says, "Watch over your heart with all diligence, For from it flow the springs of life" (cf. Deut. 6:4-7; Prov. 27:19; Matt. 15:18, 19; Rom. 5:5; 9:2; 10:9, 10).

As such, *secondly*, the heart is the source and spring of our words and actions (Prov. 4:21-23; Matt. 15:18, 19; Lk. 6:44, 45). The heart controls and is inevitably manifested by our words and actions.

Conclusion

What is it, then, to have the law written on our hearts? It is to have God's law installed in us as the ruling power of our convictions, affections, words, and actions. It is, therefore, to be convinced of its holiness and authority, delighted by its justice and goodness, and controlled by its wisdom and instruction. That, and nothing less than that, is having God's law written on our hearts.

Take the father charged with assembling a bicycle. If he is truly convinced of his need for the words, diagrams, and pictures of the instruction manual, what will he do? He will not try to put the bicycle together without consulting it. He will have a conviction that he needs it. He will be grateful when he finds the instruction manual in the box and as its instructions guide him in the assembly of the bicycle. He will carefully follow its instructions as he goes about the task of constructing the bicycle. It is even so with the man in whose heart is written the law of God. "Moreover, I will give you a new heart and put a new spirit within you; and I will remove the heart of stone from your flesh and give you a heart of flesh. And I will put My Spirit within you and cause you to walk in My statutes, and you will be careful to observe My ordinances" (Eze. 36:26, 27).[6]

What is the reason that the law is written on the heart?

Why is this writing of the law on the heart the very first act of God mentioned in the record of the New Covenant? The answer to this question is contained in verse 33 itself. ""But this is the covenant I will make with the house of Israel after those days," declares the LORD, "I will put My law within them, and on their heart I will write it; and I will be their God, and they shall be My people"" (Jer. 31:33).

Notice, *first*, the preceding phrase. After speaking of the broken Old Covenant (v. 32, "My covenant which they broke"), Jehovah returns to speaking of the New Covenant. He says, "But this is the covenant ... I will put ..." There is no covenant with God where His law is not written on the heart. The covenant is, first of all, the writing of the law in the heart. There is no participation in the New Covenant without the writing of the law in the heart. There is no knowing God, no forgiveness of sin, where there is no law written on the heart (v. 34).

Notice, *second*, the following phrase, "... and I will be their God ..." (v. 33). Pay close attention to the connecting word, "and." The promise, "I will be their God," is the essential promise of all the unfolding covenant dealings of God in the Bible. It is the promise to Abraham (Gen. 17:8). It is the promise that comes to glad fruition in the eternal state. To the son of God,

---

[6] Note that the promise of the New Covenant includes the sanctification and obedience of all its recipients. Thus, apostasy for New Covenant beneficiaries is impossible (cf. Jer. 32:40).

it is said, "I will be his God" (Rev. 21:7). The critical point is that God's law must be written on the heart if this fundamental and all-inclusive promise is to be ours. Without the writing of His law upon our hearts, God is not our God, and we are not His people.

Practical Implications

The *first* and central practical implication to be drawn from all that has been said is this: *We learn the delusion and danger of divorcing law and grace.* Law and grace must be distinguished, but they must never be divorced.

Not a few in the history of the Church have been guilty of divorcing law and grace and setting them at odds with one another. But in the last century and a half in Britain and America not a little of the blame for this problem must be laid at the feet of Classic Dispensationalism. It is a necessary and very logical outworking of that system. As we noticed in chapter one, it divides Israel and the Church and sunders the Old and the New Testament. Thus, it is no surprise that many Classic Dispensationalists divorce law and grace.

This is a serious charge. Let me substantiate it. Matthew 6:12 contains the petition of the Lord's Prayer, which goes, "And forgive us our debts, as we also forgive our debtors." Here is the comment of the old *Scofield Reference Bible*: "This is legal ground. Cf. Eph. 4:32, which is grace. Under law forgiveness is conditioned upon a like spirit in us; under grace we are forgiven for Christ's sake, and exhorted to forgive because we have been forgiven."[7] Such divorcing of

---

[7] *The Scofield Reference Bible* (New York: Oxford University Press, 1917), 1002, 1003.

law and grace is a frontal assault on the very Constitution of the Church of Christ. As we have seen, the very terms of the New Covenant require the implantation of the Divine law. The first and crucial operation of grace mentioned in the account of the New Covenant in Jeremiah 31 is the writing of the law of God in the heart. Without this, there is and there can be no grace. First Corinthians 7:19 gives us Paul's version of the same truth. "Circumcision is nothing, and uncircumcision is nothing, but *what matters is* keeping the commandments of God."

The divorcing of law and grace is a frontal assault on the very terms of the New Covenant. In light of this, several practical warnings are appropriate for us to consider.

Beware of divorcing law and grace in conversion.

Grace is perverted when it is set over against, or made the opposite of obedience to commands. Faith both rests in Christ and works through love. Though faith does not justify through its obedience to God's law, it is a kind of obedience and leads to obedience (Rom. 1:5; Gal. 5:6). When it is taught that men may be saved without confessing and submitting to Jesus Christ as Lord, that is a dangerous divorcing of law and grace in conversion. Sad to say, such teaching is not uncommon among many Evangelicals. Speaking of Jesus' conversation with the woman at the well, one such Evangelical says:

> It must be emphasized that there is no call here for surrender, submission, acknowledgement of Christ's Lordship, or anything else of this kind. A gift is being offered to one totally unworthy of God's favor. And to get it, the woman is required to

make no spiritual commitment whatsoever. She is merely invited to ask.[8]

With such teaching so prevalent, it is no wonder that we hear over and over again in Evangelical testimony meetings, "I received Jesus as my Savior first, and then several years later, I received Him as my Lord." Those who think this way have divorced grace and faith from having anything to do with practical submission to the laws of Christ, the Lord. They will even tell you that to insist on such submission for salvation is legalism and even heresy. Such teaching is a twisting of Scripture and a turning of the grace of God into license for sin. It is clearly Antinomianism.

Beware of divorcing law and grace in the regulations of your life.

This happens when men refuse to govern their lives by anything in the Old Testament law. This refusal is often justified by a false understanding of Paul's assertion that we are not under law, but under grace (Rom. 6:14). Such a divorce of law and grace manifests ignorance of two vital and basic Gospel distinctions. *First*, we are not under the law as a way of justification, but as a rule of life (Rom. 10:4). *Second*, we are not under the Ceremonial and Judicial Law as a rule of life, but only the Moral Law (Jer. 31:33; Rom. 13:8-10; Eph. 6:1-4; Jam. 2:8-11).

The tragic thing about the neglect of the Moral Law as revealed in the Old Testament and the Gospels is that the mass of biblical teaching on right conduct is found in the those parts of the Bible. No wonder the

---

[8] Zane Hodges, *The Gospel Under Siege* (Dallas: Redencion Viva, 1981), 14.

lives of so many Christians manifest so much folly, sin, and misery when modern teachers have so mutilated God's instruction manual for the Christian life.

Beware of divorcing law and grace in the motivation of the Christian life.

People sometimes say, "I want to be motivated by grace and not by the law." They think, therefore, of duty and keeping commandments as fleshly and legalistic. They believe that the only worthy reason to do God's will is because they want to or feel like it. They want to be motivated by love, not law.

There is so much wrong with such thinking that it is hard to know where to start. But certainly one thing that is wrong with such thinking is that it divorces law and grace, duty and love, and duty and desire. These things are friends, not enemies. Though God's law is written in our hearts, it is still law, torah (i.e., authoritative instruction). The words of the wisdom of God are to this effect: "The wise in heart will receive commands." "He who keeps the commandment keeps his soul."

Some think that it is ungodly, carnal, and legalistic to obey God just because He says you should, and it is your duty. The opposite is the case. Romans 8:7 says that it is the mind set on the flesh that does not subject itself to the law of God. The fact is that he who obeys just because he wants to may not be obeying God truly at all, but simply his own desires. The next time Satan comes and says to you, "You are only doing that because it is your duty," you tell him, "That's right! And I love God and my neighbor enough to do what I know I should even though I don't feel like it at times."

Beware of divorcing law and grace in dealing with the reality of sin.

The mentality here is something like this: "I don't want to live according to the law, but according to grace. So when the law reveals my sin, I will just think of God's grace and ignore it. To give way to conviction of sin is legalistic." Even if we don't say it, or think it, sometimes we respond this way to the work of the law. But this is wrong. The heart in which God's law is written must wince at the transgression of it and will not rest short of confession of sin. Thus, the experience of the ongoing confession of sin called for in 1 John 1:9 is the experience of every believer. If it is not yours, you have reason to question if God's law has ever been written in your heart.

A *second* practical implication to be drawn from all that has been said comes to us in the form of another warning. *Beware of exalting law over grace.* Law and grace, as stated above, must be distinguished, but law must never be set over grace. They go together. They complement each other in the Christian life. Law directs but grace empowers and impels the soul to keep the law. There are some tendencies that often accompany those who exalt law at the expense of grace that we must take note of and avoid.

Avoid settling for heartless obedience.

One damaging tendency among some Reformed Christians is to settle for external conformity alone. This distortion of biblical sanctification often settles for a cold, heartless approach to living the Christian life. Externals are promoted at the expense of the internal climate of the soul. Avoid settling for heartless obedience at all costs. It does not adorn the gospel. It sends the wrong message to the lost. It does not please God. It often comes when knowledge is not properly assimilated into the soul and implemented in life. It also comes when the soul losses sense of the constant necessity of the grace of Jesus Christ for *daily* living. Not only do lost souls need Jesus, but saved ones do as well! Remember Paul's words in 2 Corinthians 3:18. "But we all, with unveiled face beholding as in a mirror the glory of the Lord, are being transformed into the same image from glory to glory, just as from the Lord, the Spirit." Keep Christ at the center of your daily life and the soul will not go long in heartless obedience.

Avoid imposing on yourself or others more law than God has.

This is another damaging tendency in those who have exalted law over grace. We must stand for and approve of all the law God has for His children. We must not, however, fall into the trap of imposing upon others or ourselves more law than God has for us. This tendency, often coming from good intentions, actually does harm instead of good. It binds consciences where God does not. It often produces pride and a condescending spirit toward others. It produces pseudo guilt. Those who fall into this way of thinking often confuse God's law with things indifferent. Sometimes this is done due to the pressures of cultural norms and expectations, personal preferences, slippery slope argumentation, or long chains of logical inference from texts that do not speak to the issue being applied. Either way, it is a recipe for disaster. It does not honor God. It makes us proud; and God is opposed to the proud.

Avoid confusing law and gospel.

Those who fall into the trap of exalting law over grace often fall into another very serious error – confusing law and gospel. This happens when the Christian begins to live as if his obedience to God's law is the ground of his acceptance with God. This, in effect, turns the law into another gospel and is a practical repudiation of the work of Christ. It dishonors Christ, is a practical denial of justification by faith alone in Christ alone, cripples the soul and destroys assurance. In our zeal to uphold the law of God, we must never allow obedience to it to become our basis for initial or subsequent acceptance with God. The Lord accepts us in His beloved Son based on what He did for us and not on what we do for Him.

If God's law has been written on our heart, we will be humble. We will walk in a manner that properly balances law and grace. And when we don't, we will go to the God of the law and the God of all grace for pardon and help in our time of need.

CHAPTER THREE:
The New Covenant Constitution of the Church and Arminianism

We have compared Divine covenants to the Constitutions of nations. Yet in one respect at least they are very different. With human Constitutions, the nation already exists, and it creates by its action its own Constitution. 1987 was, for instance, the 200th anniversary of how the 13 original colonies created the Constitution of the United States of America. Even with a human Constitution, of course, there is a sense in which the 13 colonies created a new nation by their action.

With the New Covenant, it is true that it creates the nation it regulates. It is clear from the very terms of that covenant as stated in Jeremiah 31:31-34 that it is God who, by making this covenant, brings into existence the New Israel of God.

The point being addressed in speaking of the origination, building, or source of the Church is that God is, through the instrument of the New Covenant, the sole and sovereign builder, originator, and author of the Church as a whole, and of its individual members. This becomes clear through three matters clearly taught in the Bible and suggested in the passage under consideration (Jer. 31:31-34). These three points will form the outline for this chapter. They are: The Sovereign Determination behind the New Covenant; The Unbreakable Character of the New Covenant; and The Mediatorial Guarantee of the New Covenant.

The Sovereign Determination behind the New Covenant

The mere reading of verses 31-34 of Jeremiah 31 makes a tremendous impression of Jehovah's sovereign resolve in making the New Covenant. But that element of sovereign purpose and unalterable determination will be even better appreciated if we come at it by way of the very contrast suggested in our passage, the contrast between the Old and the New Covenants. In Exodus 19:4-6, the terms of the Old Covenant are stated.

> 'You yourselves have seen what I did to the Egyptians, and *how* I bore you on eagles' wings, and brought you to Myself. Now then, if you will indeed obey My voice and keep My covenant, then you shall be My own possession among all the peoples, for all the earth is Mine; and you shall be to Me a kingdom of priests and a holy nation.' These are the words that you shall speak to the sons of Israel. (Exo. 19:4-6)

With those words ringing in our minds, take note of the contrast in Jeremiah 31. In striking contrast to Exodus 19:4-6, there are no "ifs" or "maybes" in these four verses. Rather, ten times Jehovah says, "I will" or "they shall."

These verses resound with the tone of Divine certainty and sovereign determination. This tone is only strengthened by the verses that immediately follow.

> Thus says the LORD,
> Who gives the sun for light by day,
> And the fixed order of the moon and the stars for light by night,
> Who stirs up the sea so that its waves roar;
> The LORD of hosts is His name:
> "If this fixed order departs
> From before Me," declares the LORD,
> "Then the offspring of Israel also shall cease
> From being a nation before Me forever."
> Thus says the LORD,
> "If the heavens above can be measured,
> And the foundations of the earth searched out below,
> Then I will also cast off all the offspring of Israel
> For all that they have done," declares the LORD. (Jer. 31:35-37)

Jehovah makes this covenant with a sovereign determination backed by all the almighty and infinite resources of His own being. He is absolutely and wholeheartedly determined that it shall result in the salvation of His people. This is further strengthened by Jeremiah 32:40, 41. We will turn to this passage again because it supplements the predictions of Jeremiah 31 with regard to the New Covenant. But now, notice how these verses conclude these additional predictions with regard to the New Covenant. Jehovah says:

> And I will make an everlasting covenant with them that I will not turn away from them, to do them good; and I will put the fear of Me in their hearts so that they will not turn away from Me. And I will

rejoice over them to do them good, and I will faithfully plant them in this land with all My heart and with all My soul. (Jer. 32:40, 41)[1]

The Unbreakable Character of the New Covenant

Clearly, the New Covenant is not like the Old Covenant, and the point at which the difference is most plainly manifested is that the Old Covenant could be and was broken (Deut. 29:25-28; Psa. 78:10, 11; Jer. 11:9, 10; 22:6-9; 34:13, 14; Eze. 44:6-8). Note verses 31 and 32 of Jeremiah 31:

> "Behold, days are coming," declares the LORD, "when I will make a new covenant with the house of Israel and with the house of Judah, not like the covenant which I made with their fathers in the day I took them by the hand to bring them out of the land of Egypt, My covenant which they broke, although I was a husband to them," declares the LORD. (Jer. 31:31, 32)

The Old Covenant did not insure that those with whom it was made would finally gain the blessing it promised. The law written on stone could be and was broken. The Old Covenant was broken first in the sin of the golden calf. It was broken by the first generation with whom it was made at Kadesh Barnea. The whole first generation of Israel with whom that covenant was made failed to attain its blessings with the tiny exceptions of Joshua and Caleb.

But in striking contrast with a law written on stone, the writing of the law on the heart assures the keeping

---

[1] As pointed out above, the terms of the New Covenant make New Covenant apostasy impossible.

of the covenant and the certain attainment of the covenant blessings.

> "But this is the covenant which I will make with the house of Israel after those days," declares the LORD, "I will put My law within them, and on their heart I will write it; and I will be their God, and they shall be My people. "And they shall not teach again, each man his neighbor and each man his brother, saying, 'Know the LORD,' for they shall all know Me, from the least of them to the greatest of them," declares the LORD, "for I will forgive their iniquity, and their sin I will remember no more." (Jer. 31:33, 34)

Note how this is repeatedly sounded in parallel passages.

> And I will make an everlasting covenant with them that I will not turn away from them, to do them good; and I will put the fear of Me in their hearts so that they will not turn away from Me. (Jer. 32:40)

> But now He has obtained a more excellent ministry, by as much as He is also the mediator of a better covenant, which has been enacted on better promises.
> For if that first *covenant* had been faultless, there would have been no occasion sought for a second.
> For finding fault with them, He says,
> "BEHOLD, DAYS ARE COMING, SAYS THE LORD,
> WHEN I WILL EFFECT A NEW COVENANT
> WITH THE HOUSE OF ISRAEL AND WITH THE HOUSE OF JUDAH;
> (Heb. 8:6-8)

Notice the hint in Hebrews 8:8 that the problem with the first covenant was really and ultimately a problem with the people with whom it was made. The Old Covenant did not secure the covenant keeping of those with whom it was made. That was its fault. Its fault was simply that it did not enable those with whom it was made to comply with its conditions.

The purpose of Jehovah expressed in the New Covenant cannot be thwarted. It is a sovereign determination. The New Covenant cannot be broken. It is of unbreakable character. Does this mean, however, that it is unconditional? Perhaps it does, as some people define unconditional. There is an "if" in Exodus 19, but none in Jeremiah 31. But if we describe the New Covenant as unconditional, we must be very careful. The New Covenant is not unconditional in the sense that Jehovah has decided not to insist on His people fearing Him and loving His law. That is clearly just as necessary under the New Covenant as it was under the Old Covenant. It might be better to say that the New Covenant is still conditional, but with a difference. In it, God has determined so to put forth His almighty power in the hearts of His covenant people that they shall fulfill the conditions of His covenant and be the kind of men who do not break His covenant. All that the New Covenant demands it supplies.

But a question still remains. How can God simply sweep aside the demands of His own justice and make a New Covenant like this with the house of Israel after their sins have brought upon them the fierce overflowing wrath of God? Even then, in Jeremiah's day, the wrath of God was sweeping over them. How can the demands of God's holiness and justice permit Him to give such blessings as those promised in the New Covenant to men? What about their sins and iniquities? What about His justice and righteousness?

This is the great barrier between men and salvation. These questions are answered in our third heading.

The Mediatorial Guarantee of the New Covenant

Jeremiah 31:34 clearly promises that God will forget the sins of His people and forgive their iniquity, but does not tell us how a holy God can do this. We do have, however, only two chapters later in Jeremiah the seed of an answer to this problem.

> 'Behold, days are coming,' declares the LORD, 'when I will fulfill the good word which I have spoken concerning the house of Israel and the house of Judah. In those days and at that time I will cause a righteous Branch of David to spring forth; and He shall execute justice and righteousness on the earth. In those days Judah shall be saved, and Jerusalem shall dwell in safety; and this is *the name* by which she shall be called: the LORD is our righteousness.' (Jer. 33:14-16)

The Book of Hebrews brings to fruition the answer planted in Jeremiah. It enlarges on how Jesus Christ as both priest and sacrifice of the New Covenant insures and secures the establishment of the New Covenant and the impartation of its blessings to God's Israel. Note especially Hebrews 7:22, which says, "so much the more also Jesus has become the guarantee of a better covenant." As the Melchizedekian priest-king Jesus is the guarantee or surety of a better covenant. This is the only place in the New Testament where the word translated "guarantee" occurs. According to Moulton and Milligan, "[It] is common in legal and other documents."[2] It means a security, or a surety. It was even used of bailing someone out of prison. In one document there is this statement: "the father assents to the marriage and is surety for the payment of the aforesaid dowry." Another such statement is: "I hold your surety, until you pay me the value of the claims." The use of this word in the Septuagint confirms its common meaning in the world of the New Testament. Proverbs 6:1 says, "My son, if you have become surety for your neighbor, ..." and 17:18 says, "A man lacking in sense pledges, And becomes surety in the presence of his neighbor."

The meaning of this word should now be clear. The modern legal equivalent is what we know as a co-signer for a loan. Suppose a young person has landed his first good job. Now he wants to have his own car, but when he goes to the bank for a loan, he has no credit record, and the bank will not advance the money. But along comes good old dad. He has good credit, and he becomes surety by co-signing for the loan. Now what has he done by doing this? The very same thing that the surety or guarantor of Proverbs and Hebrews did. He committed himself to pay what was owed if the other person defaulted.

That is exactly what Jesus Christ did. By His blood and righteousness, He paid the debt to the justice and law of God upon which His people had defaulted. He owed nothing for Himself, but by His death He paid to the justice of God and by His life He paid to the law of God what His people owed. Because this debt is paid, the blessings of the New Covenant become a reality.

---

[2] James Hope Moulton and George Milligan, *The Vocabulary of the Greek New Testament* (Grand Rapids: Wm. B. Eerdmans Publishing Company, re. September 1985), 179.

Just as that shiny new car on the show room floor which the young person possessed only in his dreams became a reality in his driveway through the co-signing of his father, even so the blessings of the New Covenant become a reality to the people of God through the suretyship, the substitutionary curse-bearing, of Jesus Christ. All this is expounded in detail in Hebrews 10:10-19. Jesus' priestly sacrifice of Himself, once-for-all, finally, and efficaciously fulfills the demands of God's law and assures the forgiveness of sins for all who are part of the New Covenant people of God.

Concluding Lessons

We learn the truth of the doctrines of grace and the falsehood of Arminianism.

Arminianism is the system which teaches that man's free will is sovereign in salvation. The first Arminians summarized their system in five points. The idea of having a five-point summary of a doctrinal system did not begin with Calvinism.

So you will appreciate the relevance of the New Covenant to Arminianism, let's look at what its five points are.

(1) God has chosen to save those who believe in Christ and persevere in obedience to Him to the end.

(2) Christ died for each and every man, but only those who believe benefit from His death.

(3) In order for men to believe in Christ, God must work by His grace in their heart.

(4) Though this grace is the source of all good in

men, yet they may resist this grace and not be saved by it.

(5) Though God will provide everything that men need to persevere to the end, it is not certain that once a man believes in Christ unto salvation, he will persevere to the end and finally be saved.

Most Evangelicals hold to most, if not all, of these five points. They simply assume that in them the gospel itself is summarized. According to the New Covenant, however, not one of them is true. Rather, the five doctrines of grace (i.e., the Five Points of Calvinism) are, instead, the doctrine of the Bible. Let's briefly discuss them one at a time.

Total Depravity

We see the truth of total depravity in the contrast with the Old Covenant mentioned in our passage. What the Old Covenant demanded was simply faith and obedience. God had provided everything Israel could possibly need by way of external inducement to believe in Him and obey His laws, but Israel miserably failed. Israel, however, was no different than any other people. They were simply the test nation. The lesson, which the New Testament draws from the experience of Israel, is that all men are totally depraved. Romans 3:10-12, for instance, says, "There is none righteous, not even one; There is none who understands, There is none who seeks for God; All have turned aside, together they have become useless; There is none who does good, there is not even one." Every faculty of man's soul is polluted with sin. All men are unable to do anything of any spiritual good. Even repentance and faith are impossible due to this total depravity and total inability.

Unconditional Election

God's covenant is not made with a nation that has proved itself worthy of His choice. Rather, God, with sovereign, unchangeable purpose has chosen through the New Covenant to make them worthy of His choice. The Arminian idea that God chooses men, because He foresees their faith and they first choose Him, is absolutely foreign to the New Covenant. Many passages teach eternal, unconditional election (Acts 13:48; Rom. 9:14-18; Eph. 1:4; 2 Tm. 1:9).

Limited Atonement

The place at which Arminianism has most fiercely attacked the doctrines of grace concerns the atonement of Jesus Christ. Arminianism of every stripe has always claimed that Christ died for the sins of each and every man. This claim is also falsified by our study of the New Covenant.

Why do we claim that the New Covenant teaches the doctrine of limited atonement? The New Covenant is clearly the context or framework of the work of Jesus Christ. The work of Jesus Christ has no saving power divorced from the New Covenant. If anything should be clear from our studies of the New Covenant, it is that there is no salvation in any other Divine constitution or arrangement. If men are to be saved, they must be saved through the New Covenant.[3]

We have seen from the Scriptures that the cross of Jesus Christ is saving because of its connection with

---

[3] This is true of all saved prior to the death of Christ as well (Heb. 9:15; 10:1, 4).

this covenant. Jesus, in His priestly work, is the "mediator of the New Covenant" (Heb. 8:6). The Arminian doctrine of the death of Christ is that it makes salvation possible, but not certain. As priest and sacrifice, however, Jesus does not make something possible. He "guarantees" (Heb. 7:22) the New Covenant! His blood is repeatedly described in the New Testament as the blood of the covenant. Seven times the phrase "the blood of the covenant" occurs, and two more times the phrase "covenant in My blood" is used. Hebrews 13:20, 21 is representative:

> Now the God of peace, who brought up from the dead the great Shepherd of the sheep through the blood of the eternal covenant, *even* Jesus our Lord, equip you in every good thing to do His will, working in us that which is pleasing in His sight, through Jesus Christ, to whom *be* the glory forever and ever. Amen.

The blood of Jesus Christ has redeeming value because of its connection with the New Covenant, and it is only in that framework that His blood can be said to provide salvation for sinners.

Jesus' whole work was covenant work; His blood covenant blood, His priesthood covenant priesthood, His office as Mediator a covenant office. The question about the scope, extent, or design of the death of Christ ought not to be answered, therefore, without reference to this covenant. Now the question to ask is this: What is the scope, extent, and design of the New Covenant? Is it a general covenant made with everybody, making salvation possible for everyone, if they will take it? Or, is it a limited covenant made only with certain men and assuring their eternal salvation? If we are honest at all with Jeremiah 31:31-34, we will have to conclude that it is a limited covenant made with particular men and assuring their eternal salvation. If the covenant is limited and effectual, and Jesus' atonement has significance only in that context, then the atonement must be both limited and effectual for the salvation of certain men. To reach any other conclusion is to wrench the work of Christ out of its plain, biblical framework. Arminianism rips the work of Christ out of this context in which alone it has meaning, the context of a limited and particular and effectual and sovereign covenant.

Irresistible Grace

In fulfillment of His purpose, God actually writes His law upon the hearts of His people; He actually puts His fear in them. The New Covenant says nothing about God doing this, if people will let Him. If you insert that popular pet phrase of modern Evangelicalism, "if you let God," into this passage, you should admit at least that there is no justification in this passage for it. The New Covenant is full of what God does with men and not what men do with God.

Perseverance of the Saints

The idea that men can finally resist the grace of God naturally implies the Arminian doctrine that men can lose their salvation. If they can resist the grace of God before they are saved, they may still resist it afterwards. Again, the plain language of the New Covenant erases such Arminian doubts. Look again at verse 34b, "for I will forgive their iniquity, and their sin I will remember no more." If a man's sins are remembered no more, how can God ever damn him for them? But even more unanswerable are the assertions of Jeremiah 32:40. If ever a text could put to rest the contingencies that Arminians insert into the New Covenant, this text should do it. "And I will make an everlasting covenant with them that I will not turn away from them, to do them good; and I will put the fear of Me in their hearts so that they will not turn away from Me."

We learn the importance of the doctrines of grace.

The minute someone begins to preach or teach or discuss the doctrines of grace, some begin to worry about the need for balance or express concerns about extreme Calvinism. There are even those who say they believe in the sovereignty of God in salvation and in the doctrines of grace, but who will tell you that they should not be preached publicly.

How does that square with the fact that these doctrines are written large in the very terms of the New Covenant? There is no more central portion of Scripture for the Church as we have seen than that one, single passage in the entire Old Testament that explicitly mentions the New Covenant by name. The New Covenant is, as we have proven, the very Constitution of the Church. Yet in that pivotal and all-important passage, the doctrines of grace are obviously taught. There is nothing about free will emphasized in the entire passage. God's grace alone is the emphasis. Yes, we believe in the free offer of the gospel. Yes, of course, we must teach and emphasize human responsibility. All that is being said is that the New Covenant emphasizes sovereign grace publicly, and we may, and must, do the same thing.

We learn the source of the Church's growth.

Many people believe that building the Church is ultimately up to human methodologies that appeal to people who control their own salvation by their free wills. If they believe this, then there will be a great temptation to do anything that seems necessary to attract people to the Church – including turning a blind eye to one biblical teaching after another.

What will keep churches from selling out to such methods? Only the conviction that God alone is able to build His Church and that He will build it by His own appointed methods. Only the conviction that God is the one who builds His Church will keep us from abandoning His methods for the inventions of men. If God alone gives the increase (1 Cor. 3:10), then we need not pay attention to the voices that trumpet their humanistic and carnal methods of Church growth.

What are God's methods?

(1) Biblical praying. A Reformed Church without a well-attended, vibrant prayer meeting is a lie. Someone who says he believes in sovereign grace, who is not diligent in private and public prayer is, at best, terribly inconsistent and, at worst, a hypocrite.

(2) Biblical worship. This is worship that is calculated to please God not to attract the carnal multitudes.

(3) Biblical preaching. At the center of all true churches and all true gospel worship is the careful, solemn, and urgent ministry of the Word of God. Such a ministry dares to preach the whole counsel of God with prophetic power and passion.

(4) Biblical Church-life. When you take biblical
praying, worship, and preaching, and it is given
tangible expression in a well-ordered Church,
godly families, and holy lives, then you have
the weapon with which God is pleased to
advance His kingdom and Church. It takes
work, humility, tenacity to persevere in the un-
glamorous tasks that build holy churches,
families, and lives, especially when other
ministries seem so much more effective, but
this is the means appointed by God for the
advance of His kingdom.

We learn the fundamental place of the person and work of Christ in salvation.

There is no salvation to be found outside the
provisions of the New Covenant and Jesus Christ as its
Mediator. This is the great proclamation of Isaiah 42:6,
7. "I will appoint you as a covenant to the people, as a
light to the nations, to open blind eyes, to bring
prisoners from the dungeon, and those who dwell in
darkness from prison." Christ is the covenant. In taking
all He is for all you need, you have the blessings of the
New Covenant. Come to Christ for your emptiness, He
will fill you with the knowledge of God. Come to
Christ for your waywardness, He will write in your
heart the law of God. Come to Christ for your guilt, He
will give you the forgiveness of sin.

CHAPTER FOUR:
The New Covenant Constitution of the Church and Paedobaptism

In this chapter, we move from accenting the word *Reformed* to the word *Baptist*. Not only is it crucial that churches be Reformed according to the provisions of the New Covenant, it is also necessary to be Baptist, in order to be thoroughly constituted according to the New Covenant. We have asserted that the New Covenant is the Constitution of Christ's Church, and now we will seek to display that this requires the Church to be what we would call in our day Baptist.

As with each of the other chapters, we will be developing this truth in specific contrast to a doctrinal position at variance with Reformed Baptist theology. We will be interacting in this chapter with Paedobaptism. Paedobaptism is simply the technical and theological word for the practice of baptizing infants of believers.

Many revered fathers in the Christian faith, it must be acknowledged, have taught Paedobaptism. It has been taught by many whom we acknowledge as esteemed teachers in the things of God. In critiquing this doctrine, the character of such men is not being questioned. In pointing out the serious, practical dangers of Paedobaptism, no accusation is being made that Paedobaptists knowingly make the Church vulnerable to such dangers. We must acknowledge that many Paedobaptists are beloved brethren in the Lord.

That having been said, there is another necessary word of introduction. Many Christians today are Baptists, but they are so in much ignorance. They have never been acquainted with the way in which some Bible-believing Christians argue for the practice of baptizing infants. They may even assume that all Paedobaptists hold with Roman Catholics that baptism regenerates its recipients and is to be practiced because of the authoritative tradition of the Church. Such an assumption is simply wrong. It is important, then, to understand the way in which some attempt to argue from the Bible for Paedobaptism.

Interestingly enough, many, if not most, Paedobaptists openly admit that there is no clear New Testament example of an infant being baptized. They do not, at any rate, rest the burden of their position on the New Testament. Rather, they argue on the basis of the rite of circumcision. They say that since infants were circumcised in the Old Testament, then infants should be baptized in the New Testament. Since we are not to sever the Old Testament from the New Testament, since as Reformed Christians we believe that the Bible is one book, infants should be, after the example of Old Testament Israel, baptized into Christ's Church. In other words, since infants were circumcised members of God's Israel in the Old Testament, they should be baptized members of the Church, God's Israel, in the New Testament.

It must be admitted that to one familiar with the Bible, such arguments have a certain plausibility, an apparently biblical appeal. What is a proper response to such arguments? The response must not be to deny all that we have said in previous chapters about the unity of the Church and Israel, the Old Testament and the New Testament, and law and grace. That would be Dispensationalism. Any informed and instructed Reformed Christian will properly dismiss such a dispensational response to the argument for Paedobaptism. There is no need to deny that the Church is the New Israel of God or that there are certain parallels between circumcision and baptism.

The proper response to the traditional Reformed argument for infant baptism is to say that just as there is a basic unity between the Old and New Covenants, so also in the same way there is an important difference between them. As there are similarities, so there are also crucial dissimilarities. As there is continuity, so there also is discontinuity between these two covenants. And it is intensely significant that in the only passage in the Old Testament that clearly and explicitly speaks of the relationship of the Old and New Covenants, it is the differences and not the similarities that are emphasized (Jer. 31:31-34).

In opening up this chapter, we will notice three things of significance for the identity of the Church and the question of Paedobaptism: The Emphasized Dissimilarity of the New Covenant; The Precise Superiority of the New Covenant; and The Ultimate Fulfillment of the New Covenant.

The Emphasized Dissimilarity of the New Covenant

When one reads the standard Paedobaptist arguments, for example those of A.A. Hodge or Louis Berkhof, one quickly notices that they lay all the stress on the one-ness or similarity of the Old Covenant and the New Covenant. They are "identical," we are told, and baptism is simply "substituted" for circumcision.[1] The differences between these two covenants are minimized to the vanishing point.[2]

In striking contrast, Jeremiah 31 emphasizes the contrast, the difference, the dissimilarity of the two covenants (i.e., Jer. 31:31, "new"; 31:32, "not like"; Heb. 8:7, 8, the Old Covenant was not faultless and the New Covenant is.). This clear and obvious dimension of Jeremiah 31 raises profound suspicions that Paedobaptists are guilty of an imbalanced and extreme stress on the unity of the Covenant of Grace at the expense of the New Covenant. For instance, Randy Booth says, "The old and new covenants are *essentially one* [emphasis added]."[3] "The transition from the old covenant to the new covenant is a smooth unfolding of God's redemptive plan, because the two covenants are organically connected–*they are essentially one covenant of grace* [emphasis added]."[4]

> Those who insist that the new covenant is a brand-new covenant (which replaces the old covenant), as opposed to a *renewed* covenant (which *expands* the former covenant), ... The *Old Testament*,

---

[1] Louis Berkhof, *Systematic Theology* (Grand Rapids: Eerdmans, 1972), 634; A.A. Hodge, *The Confession of Faith* (Edinburgh: The Banner of Truth Trust, 1983), 346, 347.

[2] For a contemporary example of this see the appendix on Richard L. Pratt, Jr.

[3] See Randy Booth, "Covenant Transition" in *The Case for Covenantal Infant Baptism*, ed. Gregg Strawbridge (Phillipsburg, NJ: P&R Publishing, 2003), 195.

[4] Ibid., 199.

> being "old," has been set aside and invalidated, having been abrogated by the *New Testament*. ...Many places in the New Testament recognize the *complete* unity and continuity between the old and new covenants [emphases added].[5]

Notice how Booth describes the New Covenant as a *renewal* and *expansion* of the Old Covenant. This, in effect, denies the specific newness as stated by Jeremiah and is an example of an extreme stress on the unity of the Covenant of Grace at the expense of the New Covenant. "New" in Booth's thinking means *renewed* and *expanded*. The New Covenant does not insure the salvation of all New Covenant citizens; it expands and renews the Old Covenant's promises to the nations of the earth. Hebrews 8:6, however, assures us that the New Covenant is "a better covenant, which has been enacted on better promises." Notice also how Booth equates Old Testament with Old Covenant and New Testament with New Covenant. Though it is proper to state that the Old Testament contains the Old Covenant and is the authoritative document of the Old Covenant, it is not true that the New Covenant abrogates the Old Testament Scriptures. It makes the *Old Covenant* obsolete (Heb. 8:13), not the *Old Testament Scriptures*, and replaces it with the New Covenant. This is another example of overemphasizing the continuity between the covenants at the expense of their discontinuity. This prepares the way for our second point.

---

[5] Ibid., 179.

The Precise Superiority of the New Covenant

The announcement of the New Covenant in Jeremiah 31 does not, thankfully, stop with a general assertion that it is different. It goes on to tell us specifically how the New Covenant is better or superior as compared to the Old.

But here we confront a difficulty. At first glance, there seems to be nothing really new about the New Covenant. Each of its three distinctive blessings, those mentioned as that in which the covenant consists in verses 33 and 34, were possessed by Old Covenant believers. The law was written in their hearts. Describing the righteous under the Old Covenant, David says, "The law of his God is in his heart; His steps do not slip" (Psa. 37:31). The knowledge of Jehovah was theirs. Describing believers under the Old Covenant, David says, "And those who know Thy name will put their trust in Thee; For Thou, O LORD, hast not forsaken those who seek Thee" (Psa. 9:10; cf. 1 Sam. 2:12; and 3:7). The forgiveness of sins was given them. In Psalm 32:1, 2, David says, "How blessed is he whose transgression is forgiven, Whose sin is covered! How blessed is the man to whom the LORD does not impute iniquity, And in whose spirit is no deceit!" Because of such texts, many interpreters have concluded that there is really nothing new about the New Covenant. There is only, they will tell you, a *quantitative* difference between the two covenants and not a *qualitative* difference.

What is the difference between *quantitative* and *qualitative*? Take, for instance, these comments of Matthew Poole. Amidst many excellent and sensible comments on Jeremiah 31:31-34, he remarks, "Neither is it called the new covenant because it was as to the substance new, for it was made with Abraham, Gen. 17:7, and with the Jews, Deut. 26:17, 18."[6] Later, commenting on the phrase "for they shall all know me," he adds, "It is only an expression signifying the increase of knowledge, and of the fear of the Lord, that should be after the pouring out of the Spirit."[7]

The problem with such interpretations is very clear. They end up saying that the New Covenant is *just like* the Old Covenant, while the Bible says that the New Covenant is *not like* the Old Covenant (Jer. 31:32), that it is new, that it is faultless, while the other was faulty (Heb. 8:7, 8).

The key to the newness of the New Covenant is found in a phrase often overlooked even by very good interpreters. It is the words "they shall all know me" in verse 34. These words contain the major thrust of verse 34. What is the point of the emphasis of this verse? It is that while assuredly *some* knew the Lord among God's Old Covenant people, *many* did not. Witness the sons of Eli. "Now the sons of Eli were worthless men; they did not know the LORD ..." (1 Sam. 2:12). Contrast the sons of Eli with Samuel who came to know the Lord at an early age. "Now Samuel did not yet know the LORD, nor had the word of the LORD yet been revealed to him" (1 Sam. 3:7).

Because the covenant was made with the physical seed of Abraham, the physical nation Israel, and because at the early age of eight days male infants were circumcised into official membership into that physical nation, many with whom God was actually in covenant

---

[6] Matthew Poole, *A Commentary on the Holy Bible* (Edinburgh: The Banner of Truth Trust, 1975), 2:591.

[7] Ibid., 591, 592.

did not spiritually or savingly know the Lord. There were both Samuels and sons of Eli in Israel. There was Samuel before and Samuel after he heard the voice of the Lord in the holy place. There were both Davids and Joabs, both Jonathans and Abners, legally and properly circumcised into Israel, God's covenant nation.

The point of Jeremiah 31:34 is that in the New Covenant this situation would no longer obtain, would no longer be the case. Rather, speaking of His New Covenant people, His New Israel, Jehovah says, "they shall all know me." That this is one of the main aspects of the newness of the New Covenant is confirmed by what we learned about the unbreakable character of the New Covenant. In the Old Covenant, God's law was written on stone. Consequently, it could be broken, even though God had really and actually through covenant become Israel's husband (Jer. 31:32). In the New Covenant, however, the law is written on the heart of all covenant citizens, guaranteeing that no member of God's New Covenant people will ever break the New Covenant (Jer. 32:40).

Paedobaptists often speak of baptizing their children as a sign of covenant participation, but later on they have no problem speaking of the distinct possibility that those very children will opt out of or break the covenant when they come to years or become unfruitful. For instance, Randy Booth says, "Unfruitful covenant members in the old covenant were cut off, and unfruitful members in the new covenant are likewise cut off."[8] Many of them also admit that the baptism of their children does not imply that they are saved. Such assertions are, however, incompatible with the terms of the New Covenant. The

---

[8] Booth, "Covenant Transition," 197.

dictum of Scripture is that the New Covenant cannot be broken and that only genuine Christians, those who know the Lord, are in it. Remember, God says, "...I will forgive their [New Covenant Israel's] iniquities and their sins I will remember no more" (Jer. 31:34).

The fact that men must know the Lord, have God's law written in their hearts, and have their sins forgiven in order to claim a part in the New Covenant is written large across the face of the New Testament (Matt. 3:1-12; Jn. 1:12, 13; Phil. 3:3; Rom. 8:14; 9:3-5).

How does all this relate to the question of baptism and especially to Paedobaptism? Baptism is the sign of membership, the badge of participation, in the New Covenant. Yet membership in the New Covenant is restricted to those who possess its characteristic blessings. The only ground upon which one may be given the ordinances or signs of the New Covenant is that one savingly knows the Lord. Until there is biblical reason to believe that someone knows the Lord, until a person credibly professes such knowledge, there is no biblical ground to baptize them. Baptism in the absence of any saving knowledge of Jehovah is without any scriptural warrant. The baptism of an infant, or anyone else, who does not possess such knowledge is not biblical baptism.

On these biblical grounds, every form of Paedobaptism that admits that it baptizes infants who do not know the Lord is condemned. There is, however, among some Paedobaptists a theory that, at first glance, seems to meet this objection. Some Paedobaptists assert that the Bible would have us presume that the children of at least one believing parent are regenerate. They admit that occasionally in some individual cases this presumption is invalid, but they teach that God still wants us to assume that our children are regenerate. Thus, this theory would appear to conform to the requirements of the New Covenant. We baptize our infants, such people say, on the grounds that they are (presumably) regenerate.

There are a multitude of problems with this theory that become apparent upon a little reflection. The *first* one is practical. Experience shows that the infants of believers are very seldom regenerate. Even when they are, it is nearly impossible to determine until they come to riper years. To teach that the Bible would have us presume something to be true that is plainly false in the vast majority of cases is very unstable ground, indeed.

Second, we must ask these Paedobaptists where the Bible teaches this great presumption that our children are regenerate. One way in which they may respond is to tell us that children were circumcised in the Old Covenant. This response misses the whole point of Jeremiah 31. If Jeremiah 31 teaches anything, it teaches that circumcision was not given to children in the Old Covenant nation on the ground that they were regenerate, but on the ground that they were the physical seed of Abraham.

Another way in which Paedobaptists may respond is by saying that God promises in His Word to bless the means of godly parenting unto the salvation of the children of believers. "Train up a child in the way he should go and when he is old he will not depart from it." It is true that God does promise to bless and save the seed of godly parents. But this does not solve the problem for several reasons. *First*, he does not promise to save every child of godly parents without exception. *Second*, Paedobaptists bestow baptism not on the children of godly parents, but on the children of all believers on their promise that they will be godly parents. *Third*, even if God promised to save all the children of all believers, this would not mean that they would be as infants. Baptism is not to be bestowed because someone will in the future be saved, but because someone in the present displays credible evidence that they already know the Lord.

The Ultimate Fulfillment of the New Covenant[9]

One of the most crucial issues with reference to the Church is: Where shall we go for our model or picture of the Church? It is very clear in Paedobaptist literature that they find in Old Testament Israel their model for the Church. What should the Church be like, especially in its practice of baptism? The Paedobaptist answers, "It should very much like Old Testament Israel." What should baptism be like? "It should be very much like circumcision was in Israel."

The Constitution of the Church, the New Covenant, however, points us to a very different model for the Church. It points us in an opposite direction to find this model. The New Covenant holds out a different blueprint for the Church than that utilized by Paedobaptists.

The prophecy of Jeremiah 31 about all knowing the Lord is not isolated in its prediction of the universal saving knowledge of Jehovah (cf. Isa. 11:9; 52:1; 54:13; 60:21). What is the prospect set before us in such passages? It is that a day is coming in the eternal

---

[9] In Appendix 1, the concept of the final and consummate fulfillment of the New Covenant as understood by Richard L. Pratt, Jr. in *The Case for Covenantal Infant Baptism* is discussed.

state, the New Heavens and New Earth, after the second coming of Christ, when the earth will be redeemed, the Church perfected, and the wicked completely obliterated from the world. Then, verily, there shall be a perfect Church and a perfect world. Then all in the world shall know Jehovah, "from the least of them to the greatest of them" (Rev. 21:8, 27).[10] That day, however, does not commence, but rather consummates the New Covenant. Though the ultimate prospect held before us in Jeremiah 31 is that glorious day, the New Covenant has already been commenced, initiated, and inaugurated by Christ. Such predictions are already being fulfilled in an anticipatory or preliminary way in the present age and the present Church. This is plain from all the evidence we looked at in the first chapter that shows the present fulfillment of the New Covenant in the Church. It is also plain from another passage in the New Testament which cites the prophecy of Jeremiah 31:34. John 6:45 says, "It is written in the prophets, 'AND THEY SHALL ALL BE TAUGHT OF GOD.' Everyone who has heard and learned from the Father, comes to Me." Plainly, Jesus regards this prophecy as already being fulfilled during His life and ministry. You will notice, furthermore, that the reference at the beginning of the verse is to the "prophets" (plural). The reason for this is that Jesus is combining two Old Testament prophecies in the words He cites. Those two passages are Isaiah 54:13, which predicts "all your sons will be taught of the Lord," and Jeremiah 31:34, which predicts, "they shall all know Me." Thus, Jesus assumes that there is a present fulfillment of this passage as well as a future. The New

---

[10] In the New Covenant age, all in the covenant know the Lord. In the age to come, all in the world know the Lord.

Covenant is inaugurated in this age and consummated in the age to come.

How is all this relevant for the Church? We ought not to derive our model of the Church from the mixed multitude of Old Testament Israel, but from the perfected multitude of the New Jerusalem. That is the picture of the Church that we are to attempt to reproduce in our churches. That is the standard of the Church. That is what the Church should be. "All shall know me" is the banner that will fly over the New Jerusalem. It is also the sign that should be hung over the entrance to every local Church. Only those who know the Lord, that is who credibly profess to know Him, ought to be baptized and in baptism joined to the Church.

Concluding Applications

In these concluding applications, we will widen our focus and take into account the broader implications of what Jeremiah 31 teaches about Church membership or membership in the New Covenant.

We see the utter folly of placing any confidence in our having been baptized as infants into the Church or New Covenant.

Now, of course, even believers' baptism should never have been made the object of anyone's spiritual confidence. In so far as anyone has made believers' baptism a ground of spiritual hope, Jeremiah 31 utterly exposes their false hope. Christ alone and a personal relationship with Him is the only ground of confidence before God's holy throne. Nonetheless, many have persisted in thinking of baptism, especially infant baptism, as somehow bringing them into God's favor and into God's Church. Do you see the utter folly of it? Infant baptism cannot help the soul of an unbeliever, just as circumcision did not. One's infant baptism means nothing to God. What utter folly to make a rite of human invention, not ordained of God, any ground of hope for your soul or anyone else's.

We see the absolute and binding duty of being baptized as a believer.

We are not claiming that none will be saved who in ignorance of the truth is not so baptized. But it can be said to those who know the truth that baptism as a believer is a matter of obedience to Christ. Christ said, "You are My friends, if you do what I command you" (Jn. 15:14).

We see the crucial importance of maintaining biblical standards of Church membership.

This alone assures that the Church is now in some measure what it will be in the age to come. Such standards must be maintained against parental sentiment. Parental sentiment is the explanation for much of the appeal of Paedobaptist theories and the desire of parents to see their infants baptized. Such standards must also be maintained against Baptist parents who want pastors to baptize, not their babies, but their four year olds for sentimental reasons. Such standards must be maintained against the prevailing neglect of corrective Church discipline. These standards must be maintained against the prevailing easy-believism. It is the solemn duty of pastors and Church-members to maintain the standards set by the New Covenant for membership in a biblical Church.

We see the unchanging qualifications for biblical Church membership.

Those qualifications are set by the Constitution of the Church, the New Covenant. They are written plainly in Jeremiah 31:33, 34 for all to see.

> "But this is the covenant which I will make with the house of Israel after those days," declares the LORD, "I will put My law within them, and on their heart I will write it; and I will be their God, and they shall be My people. And they shall not teach again, each man his neighbor and each man his brother, saying, 'Know the LORD,' for they shall all know Me, from the least of them to the greatest of them," declares the LORD, "for I will forgive their iniquity, and their sin I will remember no more. (Jer. 31:33, 34)

We see, finally, the glorious blessing of membership in a true Church.

Authentic and legitimate membership in a true Church is a sign and seal of a blessed eternity. It is a foretaste of glory and of the marriage feast of the Lamb. In our Church fellowship, we are anticipating the fellowship of heaven. Can we think of this without feeling a sense of constraint to walk worthy in our Churches of such a privilege? What a high calling membership in a local Church is! We must exemplify the love and holiness of the New Jerusalem in our local Churches. May God help us to make our Churches more and more a foretaste of the New Jerusalem.

CONCLUSION:
A Reformed Baptist Manifesto

There is no greater need in the world today than the establishment of solid and consistently biblical churches. Such churches will be mighty pillars and supports of that truth of Christ upon which the salvation of the nations and the glory of God in the world depends. Reformed Baptists are convinced that Christ's churches must place His glory and His truth first and foremost in all things, and that because of this, in obedience to the revealed nature of the charter of the church in the New Covenant, those churches must put off Dispensationalism, Antinomianism in all its forms, Arminianism, and Paedobaptism, so that the preaching of the gospel to the nations will be unhindered. The centrality of the Church in God's plan, the importance of the Ten Commandments in the life of the believer, the precious doctrines of sovereign grace, and the necessity of knowing the Lord to be a member of the Church must be embraced in the Church and proclaimed from its pulpits. When that happens, a new day of purity and power will arrive for the gospel and the Church. May God bring that day!

APPENDIX 1
A Brief Response to Richard L. Pratt's
"Infant Baptism in the New Covenant"

Richard L. Pratt Jr. has recognized and attempted a response to the threat to Paedobaptism posed by the Reformed Baptist exegesis of Jeremiah 31:31-34 in a chapter entitled, "Infant Baptism in the New Covenant."[1] To Pratt's credit he evidences a credible understanding of the Reformed Baptist interpretation of the passage in the summary he provides at the outset of his chapter.

Pratt attempts to answer the arguments against Paedobaptism based on Jeremiah 31 (already set forth in this book) by pointing out that a comprehensive understanding of the fulfillment of this passage must take account, not just of the fulfillment in the present age, but also its fulfillment in the age to come (i.e., eternal state). Without going into all the details of Pratt's argument, it should be evident by now that the treatment of the New Covenant contained in this book is in general and hearty agreement with Pratt's insistence that the New Covenant finds its final and consummate fulfillment in the new heavens and new

---

[1] Richard L. Pratt Jr., "Infant Baptism in the New Covenant," *The Case for Covenantal Infant Baptism*, ed. Gregg Strawbridge (Philipsburg, NJ: P&R Publishing, 2003), 156-174, which is a slightly edited version of "Jeremiah 31: Infant Baptism in the New Covenant," *IIIM Magazine Online*, Volume 4, Number 1, January 7 to January 13, 2002, http://www.thirdmill.org/files/english/html/th/TH.h.Pratt.New. Covenant.Baptism.html.

earth.

Where Pratt's polemic for Paedobaptist views clearly leads him astray is in his conclusion that the New Covenant is virtually exclusively future in its establishment. Pratt admits repeatedly that the implications of the New Covenant are exactly what Baptists think, but argues that these implications are only true in the eternal state. For instance, he says:

> In the third place, we saw that many evangelicals object to infant baptism because *the new covenant distributes salvation to all of its participants.* As with the previous objections, this point of view is correct insofar as it relates to the complete fulfillment of the new covenant in the consummation.[2]

This means that for Pratt the present fulfillment of the New Covenant is merely anticipatory of its *real fulfillment* in the eternal state. This must be the case, because, for Pratt, none of its provisions are strictly fulfilled until the eternal state. In fact, in the respects that make the New Covenant *new*, it is according to Pratt's own statements akin to all the previous Divine covenants including the Mosaic Covenant.[3]

Now surely this is on the face of it a surprising conclusion for Pratt to draw. Though the New Testament teaches that there is both a present (inaugural) and future (consummate) fulfillment of the New Covenant, Pratt wants to reserve all of its distinctively new elements to the consummate state and deny them all to the inaugural state.

---

[2] Ibid., 172.
[3] Ibid., 158, 159.

What makes this conclusion even more unconvincing is that the New Testament makes clear repeatedly that the New Covenant has already been legally established or enacted. This is shown by the fact that its ordinances have been legally established (Lk. 22:20; 1 Cor. 11:25) and its officers have been legally installed (Eph. 2:20; 4:11; Heb. 8:1-6; 2 Cor. 3:6). It is also shown by the language of Hebrews 8:6 which, using the terminology of legal institution, says that it "has been enacted on better promises". James R. White speaks very pointedly to this issue:

It is important to see that for the writer, *the New Covenant has been, as a past-tense action, officially enacted.* The term used is νενομοθέτηται, the perfect passive of νομοθετέομαι, "to enact on the basis of legal sanction, ordain, found by law" (BDAG). The New Covenant is not something *that will someday be established* but has already, as a completed action, been founded, established, enacted, and that upon "better promises" than "the first" (v. 6). There is nothing in the text that would lead us to believe that the full establishment of this covenant is yet future, for such would destroy the present apologetic concern of the author; likewise, he will complete his citation of Jer. 31 by asserting the obsolete nature of the first covenant, which leaves one to have to theorize, without textual basis, about some kind of intermediate covenantal state if one does not accept the full establishment of the New Covenant as seen in the term νενομοθέτηται.[4]

---

[4] James R. White, "The Newness of the New Covenant," *Reformed Baptist Theological Review*, Volume I, Number 2 (July 2004), 156, 157.

Finally, the present (real) enactment of the New Covenant is indicated by the fact that Jesus in John 6:45 (as we have seen) cites one of the passages that is most explicitly speaking of the consummate state as already in the process of fulfillment.

For all these reasons, Pratt's conclusion strikes one as a surprisingly extreme and likely biased deduction from the consummate fulfillment of the New Covenant. A more natural conclusion to draw is the one drawn in this book. It is that the New Covenant (*de jure*) now forms the legal Constitution of the Church, even though its actual condition still resembles in some respects (*de facto*) the condition of the people of God under previous covenants.

This is the more natural explanation for a number of the passages Pratt cites in order to prove that the present people of the New Covenant is composed of both believers and unbelievers. In spite of the new legal situation that obtains through the enactment of the New Covenant, the merely inaugural fulfillment of the New Covenant means that the actual condition of the Church sometimes, and to some degree, resembles that of the mixed multitude of Israel. This is the explanation for Hebrews 10:29 and Deuteronomy 32:36 and other passages in the New Testament.

Pratt exemplifies how Hebrews 10:29 is cited frequently by Paedobaptists today. A few comments about the meaning of this passage are appropriate. The apostasy passages of Hebrews (including 10:29) are plainly speaking only of those who actually professed regeneration – not of babies supposedly born or baptized into the New Covenant. Those mentioned in Hebrews 10:29, 30 are the same as those mentioned in Hebrews 2:3, 4 and 6:4-6, where their conversion experiences are described. This is plain in John 15:1-6. Notice the contextual reference to Judas Iscariot (Jn. 13:10, 11, 30). This is plain also in Romans 11:16-24 from the fact that it is faith that grafts people into the one olive tree.

The Paedobaptist use of the apostate passages is caught on the horns of a dilemma. If they admit that the apostates are described in these passages as "sanctified" and "in Christ" because of what they professed and claimed, then it must take the position that infants may be admitted to the New Covenant only on the supposition that they are regenerate. Unless they adopt the doctrine of the presumptive regeneration of their infants, this lands them in the Baptist position of baptizing only those who profess regeneration. Since presumptive regeneration assumes that it is unnecessary to evangelize our children, is devoid of biblical support, and involves difficult logical gymnastics, most evangelical Paedobaptists hesitate to take this ground for baptizing their infants.

But the other horn of the dilemma for Paedobaptists is to argue that the language of "sanctified" and "in Christ" as used in the apostasy passages has nothing to do the profession of regeneration. These Paedobaptists argue that it merely speaks of some "covenantal" blessing really possessed by the apostates, but makes no reference to regeneration. The problems with this approach are manifold. In the *first* place, it must attribute two completely different meanings to the same words used in the same chapters. For instance, in Hebrews 10 "sanctified" must mean something completely different in verses 10 and 14 than it does in verse 29. It must also invent a merely covenantal and non-saving meaning for "in Christ" in John 15 and "by faith" in Romans 11.

But in the *second* place, the problems become even worse. Since Paedobaptists argue that this merely covenantal (but non-saving) connection to Christ is given to people through their participation in the ordinances of the New Covenant (through baptism and the Lord's Supper), they must change the meaning of baptism and the Lord's Supper. Now baptism and the Lord's Supper do not claim or profess or signify repentance and the forgiveness of sin, but only some non-saving covenantal connection to Christ. The problem, of course, with this position is that it defies the plain teaching of the entire New Testament about the meaning of baptism.

A more satisfactory interpretation of the apostasy passages is the one that argues that in them the language of profession or appearance is used. An interesting illustration of how the Bible may use the language of profession is found in 2 Chronicles 28:23. Here the King of Israel is described in terms of a profession which was plainly contrary to reality: "For he sacrificed to *the gods of Damascus which had defeated him, and said, "Because the gods of the kings of Aram helped them, I will sacrifice to them that they may help me."* But they became the downfall of him and all Israel [emphasis added]." Those mentioned in the apostasy passages are also described according to their external and visible profession and privileges, not according to inward and spiritual reality (1 Cor. 8:11; Rom. 14:15). If these passages imply that a brother can perish, such a

one is described only as to his visible profession. For
a true brother cannot perish (Rom. 14:4). Hebrews
10:29 speaks of one sanctified by the blood of Christ.
Those who are truly sanctified, however, have been
perfected forever through Christ's death (Heb. 10:10,
14), and enjoy the blessings of the New Covenant
(Heb. 10:15-18). Those mentioned in Hebrews 10:29
are only sanctified, therefore, in terms of the
language of the profession and appearance, and not in
reality.

Pratt also cites 1 Corinthians 7:14.[5] The *first*
problem with the Paedobaptist argument based on
this passage is that it proves too much. The passage
declares not only that the children are holy, but also
that the unbelieving spouse is holy (sanctified). If
such holiness provides the right to Christian baptism,
and the passage asserts that both children and
unbelieving spouses are sanctified, it would prove
that unbelieving spouses also have a right to baptism.
This is a position no Paedobaptist wishes to adopt.
The *second* problem with this interpretation is that it
ignores the context and true meaning of the passage.
Mixed marriage and divorce is the theme of the
context, not baptism, and certainly not infant
baptism. It is always precarious to deduce too much
about a given subject from a passage that is not
dealing with that subject. The *third* problem with this
interpretation is that once the real meaning of this
passage is understood that meaning completely
destroys any supposed support it gives to infant
baptism. The context makes clear that believers in
Corinth were being tempted to send away their

---

[5] Pratt, "Infant Baptism in the New Covenant," 171, 172.

unbelieving marriage partners. Hence, Paul admonishes them not to do this (vv. 12 and 13). Then in verse 14 Paul addresses the reasoning by which some Corinthian Christians were justifying divorcing their unbelieving spouses. The premise, foundation, or starting point is only stated in the last clause of verse 14 that, significantly, begins with the explanatory conjunction "for". That premise is the assumed holiness and clean-ness of the children of such marriages. Paul assumes that those who were rationalizing the divorce of unbelieving spouses do not want to say that their offspring are illegitimate (unclean). The point of the passage is that if the children of a marriage are holy (i.e. clean or legitimate) then the marriage must be a proper marriage. Paul is saying to the rationalizing Corinthians that *when* they are willing to call their children illegitimate, *then* they may think of their marriages as illegitimate. It is illogical, he tells them, to want legitimate children, but an illegitimate spouse or marriage. In other words, the same argument, which justifies divorcing their spouses, also leads to the conclusion that their children are illegitimate or unclean. Only when they can stomach this conclusion may they use the argument that leads to it. The terms, holy or holiness, were used in this way (to refer to what we call legitimacy or illegitimacy) in Jewish literature. Clearly, the fact that certain children are the legitimate offspring of a legitimate marriage has nothing whatever to do with any supposed covenant holiness or a right to Christian baptism.

By way of conclusion, a number of problems with Pratt's argument may be summarized. *First*, he draws an unlikely and extreme conclusion from the

consummate fulfillment of the New Covenant in the
eternal state. His basic argument is that the promises
of the New Covenant will not be fully realized in the
covenant community until the eternal state. Until
then, the covenant community will be a mixed
community, as it has been all along. In this schema,
nothing changes, at least during the interadvental
period. As with the Old Covenant, so with the New
Covenant: some break the covenant, some don't;
some have the law written on their hearts, some
don't; some have their sins forgiven, some don't.
Pratt's argument seems to strip the New Covenant of
any newness whatsoever. *Second*, a more natural
implication of the distinction between the inaugural
and consummate fulfillment tends to support the
Reformed Baptist position. *Third*, he uses
controversial passages capable of alternative
interpretations to support his unlikely conclusion.
Fourth, he ignores the many passages – some cited in
this book – that confirm that in the present era of
fulfillment of the New Covenant only the regenerate
are in it and have a right to its ordinances.

APPENDIX 2
New Covenant Theology,
Tom Wells and Fred Zaspel
(Frederick, MD: New Covenant Media, 2002),
reviewed by Richard C. Barcellos[1]

Tom Wells and Fred Zaspel are to be commended for their work entitled *New Covenant Theology: Description, Definition, Defense* (*NCT*). It is a very irenic presentation of New Covenant Theology and well documented. I am thankful to the authors for providing us with a book that advances the important discussion among Calvinistic Baptists regarding the law and the covenants.

While reading *NCT*, I learned some new things and was reminded of other noteworthy facts about New Covenant Theology. All New Covenant Theology adherents do not equate the Decalogue with the Old Covenant. John Reisinger held this view for many years. It formed the main thesis of his influential *Tablets of Stone*. Reisinger has made it known recently on his website that he no longer holds this view. As well, I learned that I misrepresented Fred Zaspel in my book *In Defense of the Decalogue* (*NCT*, 188, n. 263). I stand corrected and regret this careless, though not intentional misrepresentation. I was reminded that New Covenant Theology relies heavily on a certain understanding of Matt. 5:17-48, especially v. 17. Finally, I learned some new things

[1] Used by permission from *Reformed Baptist Theological Review*.

about New Covenant Theology and its perspective on the nature of moral law. I will limit my critique to the following issues: *NCT* and Matt. 5:17-48; *NCT* and moral law; and *NCT* and *In Defense of the Decalogue* (*IDOTD*).

Fred Zaspel discusses what appears to be the exegetical lynchpin of *NCT* in chapters five through eight. His discussion surrounds what Douglas J. Moo (on the back cover) calls "the pivotal Matthew 5:17-20." Zaspel himself acknowledges this:

> Indeed, the whole NT theology of law grows out of this pivotal statement of Jesus. It is of "primary importance in trying to understand Jesus' attitude to the law" [quoting D. A. Carson] and, consequently, in developing a consistent theology of law and its relation to the Christian. (*NCT*, 78)

NCT bases its subsequent exegetical and theological discussion on Zaspel's interpretation of Matt. 5:17-20, which is dependent upon D. A. Carson. Greg Welty has written a critical analysis of their view entitled: Eschatological Fulfillment and the Confirmation of Mosaic Law (A Response to D. A. Carson and Fred Zaspel on Matthew 5:17-48). It is available on the Internet at: *www.ccir.ed.ac. uk/~jad/welty/carson.htm.*

Welty demonstrates that their interpretation of πληρόω (fulfill, Matt. 5:17) is implausible and that the subsequent application of this concept to the antitheses of Matt. 5:21-48 is contradictory. Welty argues, and I think persuasively, that Carson's interpretation of πληρόω is a novelty in Matthean usage. Carson claims that Jesus' ethical teaching fulfills what is foreshadowed in Moses' law. Welty acknowledges that several times πληρόω refers to Christ's person or actions fulfilling OT prophecy. But he also demonstrates that πληρόω never refers to OT laws being fulfilled by Jesus' teaching or, as Welty states it, "laws fulfilling laws."

Zaspel's thesis revolves around the meaning of one word, πληρόω. He claims that it is "the key word to the entire discussion" (*NCT*, 111). The 'entire discussion,' in the context of Zaspel's statement, refers to Matt. 5:21-48 as well. Putting such stock in the meaning of one word is hermeneutically dangerous and may be theologically disastrous. If Zaspel's interpretation of πληρόω is found wanting, then suspicion must be cast upon the validity of *NCT's* main arguments, since so much of its subsequent discussion relies on the meaning of this word.

Zaspel says, "With all the press Matthew gives to this word (*pleroo*), the question of definition becomes greatly simplified" (*NCT*, 111). What follows in the book are eight pages dedicated to defining this one word. He concludes that πληρόω means that "Jesus came to bring about what Moses' law anticipated" (*NCT*, 118). "Just as Moses' law advanced the law which God had 'written on the heart' of man at creation, so also in Jesus' teaching that advance is brought to full completion" (*NCT*, 118). It is of interest to note that no exegesis is provided for this claim. Zaspel does footnote one of his pamphlets at this point. This understanding of the advancement of law throughout redemptive history, however, is such a crucial and pivotal element of *NCT's* view of the law that making a passing reference to this leaves the critical reader wondering. Where does the Bible teach that Moses' law advanced the law that God had written on the heart of man at creation, in the sense intended by Zaspel? Could this have come from the authors' view of πληρόω infused back into the OT? For the record, Reformed theology teaches that the law written on the heart at creation was 'advanced' by the law written on stones at Sinai in *clarity* and *perspicuity*, though not in *essence* and *spirituality*. It is the same law revealed in a different manner. The advance is not one of *quality* but of *clarity* due to the presence of sin in man's heart. Is this not what Jesus is doing in Matt. 5:17-48? He is making clear what had become obscure through the sinful teachings of the Pharisees.

NCT's understanding of πληρόω may be labeled the eschatological advance view. "It is not that Moses is set aside so much as he is 'fulfilled' by the advance Jesus gave him" (*NCT*, 87). This concept of eschatological advance is then applied to the antitheses of Matt. 5:21-48. As Zaspel examines the antitheses, he finds several nuances of eschatological advance: Matt. 5:21-22, "some sort of advance …extension or addition" (*NCT*, 105); Matt. 5:27-28, "advance of some sort" (*NCT*, 105); Matt. 5:31-32, "another advance …a tightening …an abrogation" (*NCT*, 106); Matt. 5:33-34, "obsolete" (*NCT*, 106); Matt. 5:38-39, while Jesus may not formally repeal the lex [law], he very severely restricts its use" (*NCT*, 107); Matt. 5:43-44, "Jesus extends the law's requirement. Simply put, Jesus demands more than Moses" (*NCT*, 107). Zaspel claims that the view, which understands Jesus as correcting Pharisaic casuistry, does not fit the evidence (*NCT*, 108). According to Zaspel, the antitheses are not contrasting Pharisaic teaching with the Law of Moses but the Law of Moses, on the main, with the Law of Christ, thus illustrating his understanding of πληρόω. Zaspel closes his discussion of the antitheses with these words:

> …it seems that Jesus, 1) claims an authority that is superior to that of Moses; and 2) exercises that authority by taking the law of Moses in whatever direction he sees fit. In some cases, he leaves the particular command intact (#1 and 2). In other cases he extends the teaching of the command as originally given or advances it in some other way (#1, 2, 3?, 6). In still other cases he seems to rescind the original legislation (#3, 4) or at least restrict it (#5). (*NCT*, 108)

In ethical contexts, πληρόω refers to obeying and upholding the law as stated (cf. Rom. 8:3; 13:8-10). Nowhere in the rest of the NT do we see the phenomenon of eschatological advance as necessitated by Zaspel's interpretation. If the law of Christ is all the commands of the NT plus those things in the OT "that are moral laws in light of the NT" (*NCT*, 75), as Wells claims, and if the law of Christ was anticipated by and advanced beyond the law of Moses, then why don't we see this phenomenon in the rest of the NT? Indeed, what we see is direct quotations of the very law that is supposedly advanced, and that without qualification (cf. Eph. 6:2-3; Jam. 2:8-11). It appears that *NCT* confuses moral law with positive law (see below).

Zaspel's understanding of πληρόω in Matt. 5:17 is a novelty in Matthean usage, complicates the antitheses unnecessarily, and does not find support in other NT ethical contexts where the word is used to refer to the law and its New Covenant fulfillment.

While discussing moral law, Wells says, "Whatever is moral binds all men at all times" (*NCT*, 176, n. 253). With this I agree. On the next page, however, he says, "We must not, then, make Christ look and sound very much like Moses in his approach to moral law" (*NCT*, 177). I find this difficult, if not impossible, to reconcile with his previous assertion about the universality of moral law. Wells defines moral law as follows:

> Moral law is the law that has its source in the unchanging moral character of God with the result that it is intrinsically right and therefore binds all men of every era and land to whom it comes. (*NCT*, 162)

Wells adds, "moral law is found wherever there is a revelation of the moral character of God" (*NCT*, 162). But then he asks, "Is the revelation of God's character progressive?" (*NCT*, 162). He proceeds to base moral law on the progressive nature of special revelation. Since God reveals His character progressively in the Bible, moral law is revealed progressively. In other words, he argues for a dynamic concept of moral law. Indeed, he even claims that we will not know *the* moral law until the eternal state (*NCT*, 164, 166). Is this not a bit speculative? Reformed theology, however, bases its understanding of moral law on creation *imago Dei*. When God made Adam, he made him to be like Himself, to reflect His communicable attributes. Creation *imago Dei* involves having the law of God written on the heart (Rom. 1, 2). It is that law which is based on God's character. In another place, Wells says that "all law from God came with moral force" (*NCT*, 164). He appears to base moral law upon God's will *and* His unchanging character. He makes no distinction between positive law and moral law. Positive law includes any laws added to the natural law (i.e., law of creation or moral law) due to the entrance of sin and is based on God's will and is man's possession via special revelation (i.e., Scripture). Moral law is based on creation *imago Dei* and on God's unchanging nature and is man's possession via general revelation and, due to the entrance of sin, Scripture. Positive law is dynamic throughout redemptive history; moral law static. Wells appears to infuse Zaspel's understanding of πληρόω into his discussion of moral law. This has detrimental implications for the identity of the law written on the heart (i.e., natural law), the basis of the Covenant of Works, the perpetuity of moral law, the Sabbath, the active obedience of Christ, and the imputation of righteousness.

In the preface, the authors state that "the occasion that prompted this volume was the publication of a book containing a friendly but serious attack on NCT" (*NCT*, 1). They are referring of course to my book. Though they chose not to interact with it on all fronts, something for which I do not fault them, I was happy to see that they devoted specific interaction in chapters 11 and 12. I was rather perplexed, however, that they did not deal with Jer. 31:31-34 and my exposition of it in any depth. Wells makes a somewhat cavalier dismissal of my interpretation and then makes a very confusing statement. He says, "Barcellos argues at length that the law in Jeremiah 31:33 is the Decalogue (pp. 16-24). I suspect that this is too constricting and that the law there is the full Mosaic law" (*NCT*, 170, n. 246). I would expect him to say that my view is too constricting. But I would not expect him to imply that Jeremiah meant that God would write *the full Mosaic law* on the hearts of New Covenant saints. This appears to contradict the main thesis of Zaspel's argument from Matt. 5:17, unless of course one reads Zaspel's argument back into Jeremiah. This seems a bit hermeneutically strained.

Jer. 31:31-34 and its corroborating New Testament witnesses are foundational to the issues at stake. The text in Jeremiah discusses both the New Covenant and the law. For this reason we should expect this text to get more exegetical attention in a book entitled *New Covenant Theology*. In fact, the pivotal biblical passage of the entire book, Matt. 5:17-48, though it discusses law, does not discuss the New Covenant, at least explicitly. In hermeneutics, it is always safest to start with the explicit words of Scripture pertaining to the issues at stake. *NCT's* theological methodology leaves room for improvement at this point since it is established upon shaky hermeneutical and exegetical grounds.

While discussing my exposition of Matt. 5:17-20, Wells says:

> I suspect our author shows here that he has confused the NCT position with some views of classical Dispensationalism. ...Barcellos, however, must not attribute these things to NCT as he seems to do by repeating the words "this view" throughout pages 62-63. (*NCT*, 200)

For the record, I was intending older Dispensationalism by the phrase 'this view.'

While discussing my exposition of 1 Tim. 1:8-11, Wells points out several observations and disagreements (*NCT*, 190-199). The reader is encouraged to read my article in the *Reformed Baptist Theological Review* I:1 (January 2004). It has been considerably edited and expanded since the publication of the book.

In an appendix, "John Bunyan on the Creation Sabbath," Zaspel provides an extended quote from Bunyan (*NCT*, 293-294). No explanation is provided concerning what is being argued by this quotation. He prefaces Bunyan's words with these: "Bunyan responded more thoroughly." What we are not informed of is the context and reason for which Bunyan says what he does. The quote in question comes under this heading: "Whether the seventh day Sabbath, as to man's keeping of it holy, was ever made known to, or imposed by, a positive precept upon him until the time of Moses? which from Adam was about two thousand years" (John Bunyan, *The Works of John Bunyan* [Carlisle, PA: The Banner of Truth Trust, 1991], 2:363). The full title of Bunyan's treatise is "Questions about the Nature and Perpetuity of the Seventh-Day Sabbath and Proof that the First Day of the Week is the True Christian Sabbath" (Ibid., 2:359). In *IDOTD* I attempted to show that Bunyan was arguing against the perpetuity of the *seventh-day* Sabbath from creation to consummation (*IDOTD*, 100-107). Ample references from Bunyan were provided to prove that he did not believe the *seventh-day* Sabbath was moral but that "a Sabbath for holy worship is moral" (Bunyan, *Works*, 2:361). Elsewhere, Bunyan says, "it is evident that the substance of the ten commandments was given to

Adam and his posterity" (Bunyan, *Works*, 1:499). It is very evident that Bunyan held that the Sabbath as moral law predated the tablets of stone but that the *seventh-day* Sabbath began with the positive laws attending the Old Covenant. It is unclear to me what Zaspel was seeking to prove by this appendix. If he was attempting to prove that Bunyan did not believe that the *seventh-day* Sabbath predated Moses, then I agree with him. If he was attempting to prove that Bunyan did not believe the Sabbath is moral law and rooted in creation, then I disagree with him.

While reading *NCT*, I was reminded that the issue of the Sabbath is not the only thing upon which we differ. New Covenant Theology adherents often tout this as the only difference between us. Reading *NCT* convinced me that, though we differ on the Sabbath, our differences cut much deeper than this subject alone. Those differences are exegetical, theological, and historical. It is improper, therefore, for those on either side of this issue to claim that the Sabbath is the only issue dividing us.

I would like to close on a positive note. Through various circumstances, I have come to know Tom Wells on a personal level and consider him to be a dear, highly esteemed brother in the Lord. We have had several friendly, challenging, and edifying email exchanges and phone conversations. I am sure that this would be true of many other New Covenant Theology adherents and trust that this review will be taken as constructive criticism from a differing friend and brother.

BIBLIOGRAPHY

The bibliography includes books cited and recommended reading for the subjects discussed. The recommended reading books are preceded by *. Some titles may be out of print or available from other publishers.

*Barcellos, Richard C. *In Defense of the Decalogue: A Critique of New Covenant Theology*. Cape Coral, FL: Founders Press, 2001.

*———. *Paedoism or Credosim? (A Reformed Baptist Argument For Baptism of Believers Only)*. Fullerton, CA: Reformed Baptist Publications, nd.

Blaising, Craig and Bock, Darrell. *Progressive Dispensationalism*. Grand Rapids, MI: Baker Book House Company, 2002.

*Chantry, Walter. *Baptism and Covenant Theology*. Fullerton, CA: Reformed Baptist Publications, nd.

*———. *Imputation of Righteousness & Covenant Theology*. Fullerton, CA: Reformed Baptist Publications, nd.

*———. *Signs of the Apostles: Observations on Pentecostalism Old and New*. Carlisle, PA: The Banner of Truth Trust, 1973, 1987.

*———. *Today's Gospel: Authentic or Synthetic?* Carlisle, PA: The Banner of Truth Trust, 1970, 1985.

*Haykin, Michael A.G. *Kiffin, Knollys and Keach: Rediscovering our English Baptist Heritage*. Leeds, England: Reformation Today Trust, 1996.

*Howell, R.B.C. *The Covenants*. Wilmington, OH:

Hampton House Books, 1855, re. 1991.

* Jewett, Paul K. *Infant Baptism & The Covenant of Grace.* Grand Rapids, MI: William B. Eerdmans Publishing Company, 1978, 1980.

*Kevan, Ernest F. *The Grace of Law: A Study of Puritan Theology.* Grand Rapids, MI: Baker Book House, 1976, 1983.

*Malone, Fred A. *The Baptism of Disciples Alone: A Covenantal Argument for Credobaptism Versus Paedobaptism.* Cape Coral, FL: Founders Press, 2003.

*Martin, Robert P. *Accuracy of Translation and the New International Version.* Carlisle, PA: The Banner of truth Trust, 1989.

*———. *The Death Penalty: God's Will or Man's Folly?* Avinger, TX: Simpson Publishing Company, 1992.

*Murray, Iain H. *The Forgotten Spurgeon.* Carlisle, PA: The Banner of Truth Trust, 1966, 1986.

*Murray, John. *Principles of Conduct.* Grand Rapids, MI: Wm. B. Eerdmans Publishing Company, 1957, 1999.

*———. *Redemption Accomplished and Applied.* Grand Rapids, MI: Wm. B. Eerdmans Publishing Company, 1955, 1987.

Pentecost, J. Dwight. *Things to Come.* Grand Rapids, MI: Zondervan Publishing House, 1964, 1979.

*Pink, Arthur W. *The Sovereignty of God.* Carlisle, PA: The Banner of Truth Trust, 1961, 1986.

*Pipa, Joseph A. *The Lord's Day.* Fearn, Ross-shire, Great Britain: Christian Focus Publications, 1997.

*Robertson, O. Palmer. *The Christ of the Covenants.* Phillipsburg, NJ: Presbyterian and Reformed Publishing Co., 1980, 1985.

———. The Israel of God: Yesterday, Today, and Tomorrow. Phillipsburg, NJ: P&R Publishing, 2000.

Ryrie, Charles Caldwell. *The Basis of the Premillennial Faith.* Neptune, NJ: Loizeaux Brothers, 1975.

Saucy, Robert L. *The Case for Progressive Dispensationalism: The Interface Between Dispensational & Non-Dispensational Theology.* Grand Rapids, MI: Zondervan Publishing House, 1993.

*Savastio, Jim. *What is a Reformed Baptist Church?* Avinger, TX: Simpson Publishing Company, 2003.

*Seaton, Jack. *The Five Points of Calvinism.* Carlisle, PA: The Banner of Truth Trust, 1970, 2000.

*Stander, H.F., and Louw, J.P. *Baptism in the Early Church.* Garsfontein, South Africa: Didaskalia Publishers, 1988, 1994.

Strawbridge, Gregg, ed. *The Case for Covenantal Infant Baptism.* Phillipsburg, NJ: P&R Publishing, 2003.

The Baptist Confession of Faith of 1689.

The Shorter Catechism: A Baptist Version. Avinger, TX: Simpson Publishing Company, 1991, 2003.

*Waldron, Samuel E. *A Modern Exposition of the 1689 Baptist Confession of Faith.* Durham, England: Evangelical Press, 1989, 1995.

*———. *Baptist Roots in America: The Historical Background of Reformed Baptists in America.* Avinger, TX: Simpson Publishing Company, 1991.

*———. *Biblical Baptism: A Reformed Defense of Believers Baptism.* Grand Rapids, MI: Truth for

Eternity Ministries, 1998.

*———. *The End Times Made Simple*. Amityville, NY: Calvary Press, 2003.

*Warfield, Benjamin B. *The Plan of Salvation*. Avinger, TX: Simpson Publishing Company, re. 1989, 1997.

*Wells, Tom. *A Price for a People: The Meaning of Christ's Death*. Carlisle, PA: The Banner of Truth Trust, 1992.

*Welty, Greg. *A Critical Evaluation of Infant Baptism*. Fullerton, CA: Reformed Baptist Publications, nd.

*White, James. *The Potter's Freedom*. Amityville, NY: Calvary Press, 2000.

Scripture Index

General Index